What Peop

The Unir

*My Journey from Spiritually-Starved Workaholic
to Connecting to "All That Is"*
(the story of creating The New I AM Document)

"A magical journey of inspiration and human perseverance, told by a magnificent, powerful, and gracious being. Janie shares in a way that comes truly from the heart and moves the soul. A definite must-read."

JB Owen
Founder and CEO of Ignite
www.igniteyou.life

"Janie J gives the reader a snapshot of her life as it unfolded and her spiritual journey began. Follow along as you learn just how much her life changed and affected every aspect of her being. Be inspired to start on your own soul path."

Don Boyer
Film Producer
www.BeyondtheSecret.com

"If you want to find answers to those pesky life issues that have plagued you for years, Janie's book will teach you how to learn your life lessons, access your own higher intuitive guidance, and get out of your comfort zone so you can have the life you want. Charming and succinct, The Unimagined Awakening is a wonderful guide to the next stage of your soul's journey!"

Dr. Gary Salyer
Transformational Relationship Mentor, Speaker & Author
www.garysalyer.com

"Rather daring! This story takes us beyond what we might expect. It was fascinating to watch the massive transformation - a true transformation - spiritually and lifewise. A story worth reading and experiencing!"

Keith Garrick
Author and Creator of The Life University
www.thelifeuniversity.us

"Janie's message comes to you fresh from a realm beyond our everyday perception. This is why she was chosen to deliver it to us. Only read if you want to awaken, and if you want to awaken, read every word!"

Yoram Baltinester
The Personal Development Samurai
International Best-Selling Author
www.HeyYoram.com

"Janie Jurkovich is so spot on in how we land here with lessons. Can we learn our lessons faster? Yes, we can, by paying attention and the wisdom of this book in your hands right now will help you clue in to the lessons handed to us ever so subtly."

Rusti L Lehay
Book Coach/Empathic Editor
International Best-Selling Author

The New
I AM Document

Volume 1

Also by Janie Jurkovich:

Live the Life You Have Imagined

Live the Life You Have Imagined: Companion Journal

Single and Sixty

Ignite Your Adventurous Spirit (Contributor)

The Unimagined Awakening:
My Journey from Spiritually-Starved Workaholic to
Connecting to "All That Is"

The New
I AM Document

Volume 1

A compilation of spiritual downloads
from
Ascended Masters (Archangels)

Transcribed by Janie Jurkovich

Golden Spiral Press

The New I AM Document—Volume 1: A compilation of spiritual downloads from Ascended Masters (Archangels)

Copyright © 2021 by Janie Jurkovich

Published by Golden Spiral Press
2491 Alluvial Ave, Ste 120
Clovis, CA 93611

goldenspiralpress.net

ISBN # 978-1-7369476-3-0

First Printing, December 2021

Printed in the United States of America

Cover Image by merznatalia via 123rf.com

ACKNOWLEDGEMENTS

The writing of this book was greatly improved by the assistance of others. This is an example of how we are all connected, and it is our responsibility to work together to help lift mankind to a new way of thinking.

My son—even though doubtful in the beginning of my capabilities as a medium—nonetheless agreed to help edit the book. We spent time on family holidays going over the lessons. This was remarkable especially considering his first language was not English. My hat is off to you, Bradley Doak!

The layout of this publication is a result of the meticulous efforts of Bryan Pfeifer. This tedious job (to my way of thinking) was handled with smooth professionalism and is very much appreciated.

My photographer, Wonda Correia of Signature Creations, once again captured the magical setting where my journey began as well as showing me in a more subdued manner more congruent with the lessons I was called to share with the world. She has the capability of always showing me in the brightest light.

My book editor and marketer extraordinaire, Beth Bridges, tirelessly reviewed this book for spelling, grammar, and consistency. Not much rewriting or editing is required when the Ascended Masters are dictating it!

My spirit guides have repeatedly told me, "We are all but cogs in the wheel of creation, each doing our own part to move mankind forward." I truly appreciate the efforts of these individuals to bring my life's mission to print.

My goal is that all mankind learns from their example that we all are truly and deeply connected.

TABLE OF CONTENTS

INTRODUCTION

Greetings fellow mankind. My name is Janie J and I am a "medium" or "channeler."

For those of you unfamiliar with what that means (like I used to be), it means I am able to connect between the spirit realm, which we can sense but not see, and our physical world here on Earth.

I learned how to do this a few years ago when I kept asking and trying to connect to a very special person in my life. I had no idea that such a deep desire would have this outcome!

I have used this gift to connect to many souls—living and deceased—in order to gain understanding and to help them and their families. This ability can be "turned on" quite easily by simply asking them.

Other times it can be a bit intrusive and I can hear or sense these souls speaking to me without provocation on my part.

I believe they can tell I'm an open channel and able to sense their feelings. Again, it is quite informative. I have learned many important lessons this way.

[Editor's Note: You can learn this method by downloading the author's Connect to Transform Process™ PDF for free at www.TheNewIAMMovement.com/transform]

INTRODUCTION

At the end of 2016, I was told to write three books, which I did along with strict deadlines. However, the publishing of those books was a bit slow on the execution. The purpose of these books is to encourage women to live their best lives.

Another book is also in the making, designed to open up women to the possibility of a spiritual life – for living one's best life does indeed include spirituality, which is nothing more than the understanding that there is more to life than what we experience in the physical world here on Earth.

In early 2019, I was given my final life's mission. (Yes, we *really* do have one!) That mission is to transcribe a document that is known as, "The New I AM Document."

By transcription, I mean, I sit quietly and these words, these teachings, come to me from above...from Ascended Masters (or Archangels) assisting God. This book is the first of three discourses.

This mission will carry me through until the end of my earthly life—into my late 90's.

It's important to know that as a child I received very little religious training. Often, I would sense "right or wrong," yet it would be nothing specifically learned from my parents.

An example I remember vividly is being in middle school where social cliques were prevalent. To talk to an outsider was reason for you to be excluded, which I quickly discovered.

This never seemed "right" to me. I know now that this lesson was embedded inside me when I began life on Earth.

Another long-held belief of mine has been that it doesn't matter if you succeed on a specific task. It matters most that you try your best. This belief was not instilled in me by my parents or teachers. Now I know this belief also came with me, as you will learn the same lesson in this book many times.

I ask that you listen carefully with an open mind and an open heart, to my transcriptions.

Absorb them into your being and strive to teach others through your actions and words, so that someday all mankind will be lifted up to a new way of life, a new reality where we are all truly and deeply connected *and* aware of such connectedness.

Be well. Be love. Be the light.

Janie J

INTRODUCTION

UNIVERSAL TRUTHS

Those who achieve greatness were willing to suffer the stigma.

You are capable of achieving your most magnificent dreams.

Dreams really do come true.

Your best days are ahead.

You can dream it. You can do it.

The power of positivity cannot be underrated.

You are special in the eyes of God.

Miracles do happen.

You are worth it.

You are a magnificent being, quite capable of greatness.

You are the World to someone. Be that Someone to another.

The greatest gift is Kindness.

Be Kind to those in need.

Empathy and Compassion are great traits to possess.

Be kind and loving to others.

Judging is reserved for God.

Have an open mind and an open heart.

Life is a playground for learning. Pay attention!

Your darkest days are behind you.

Always do your best.

Your best is all that God requires.

The Kingdom of God awaits those who believe.

Believe in yourself before others will believe in you.

Encouragement is our duty to others.

Be the light. Show others the way.

Remember to Smile.

Kindness, Compassion and Understanding can be felt, not heard.

Remember to be the kind and loving person you were created to be.

Brighten someone else's life and it will brighten yours.

Ask and It is Given.

Life is a journey, not a destination.

You are perfect just as you are.

Ask, Believe, be Grateful and Wait—the keys to Manifestation.

You can make all your wishes come true.

Words are important. Choose wisely.

Being in nature heals you.

You are deserving of all your dreams.

Believing can make it so.

Believe in You!

You are worthy of great things.

The answers are within You.

Religions are steppingstones to Understanding.

Pay attention to the Lessons in Life.

You will repeat what you do not learn; so, pay attention!

Be Grateful, always.

You will reap as you sow; so, plant wisely.

Your every deed does not go unnoticed.

Step up in boldness and seek your truth.

We all are special in God's eyes.

Look for the good in others.

Your kindness will reverberate far past what you can see.

Envision your future and make it so.

We are all capable of greatness.

Live not in the past, but with an eye to the future.

Your happiness is *your* responsibility.

No one can make you unhappy but you.

We all have free will. Do not give yours away.

In the end all will be known. Just Trust.

See the goodness in others.

Enjoy the little things.

We all have much to be grateful for.

Seek Understanding; seek the Truth; and you will find both.

Listen more. Talk less.

Always be mindful.

Your dreams create your destiny.

Dream big. Then dream even bigger.

Your destiny is your doing.

Create your dreams and create your future.

Do not let the worries of others hold you back.

Worrying is a waste of time.

Your efforts equal your results. Don't shortchange yourself.

If someone told you: you could have, be or do anything—would you believe?

Another person's opinion of you is none of your business.

Listen to your heart.

The body tells what the soul cannot.

Be gentle with the soul of another.

The world needs more kindness.

Kindness, compassion, and empathy are traits of the learned.

Your actions speak volumes, much more than your words.

Do your part to spread love, kindness, joy, and hope.

For the flower to grow, a seed must first be planted.

Be strong for you are stronger than you know.

The Universe has your back, so stand tall and walk with determination and strength.

Your dreams and wishes CAN come true.

Believing can make it so.

Love conquers all.

The strongest power in the Universe is Love.

Love never dies, it is merely transformed.

Accept others as they are and as you wish to be accepted.

Everyone has value. It's not our job to decide how much.

Love is giving. Love is magical. Love is everlasting.

Just when you think you've loved all you can, God will give you the opportunity to love even deeper.

Be not afraid to love deep, love true and love always.

Vulnerability is the key to discovering your truth.

Be positive. It's infectious.

Negativity has no place in your mind.

Negativity is a physical "thing." Do not pass it to another.

Good health = a good life.

Your health is *your* responsibility.

Feed your body and your mind with proper fuel.

Lesson 1 - The Purpose

In the beginning, God created the Heavens and Earth as a playground, much like a classroom for mankind to learn and grow, to become all he/she can be.

The purpose was the growth or Ascension of mankind to the next level of evolution where all men/women are all-knowing and very much aware of their connectedness to each other and to the Earth—to include the environment and all the animals. We *are* all truly connected as One; much, much more than the individual man knows at this moment.

All mankind has different issues to handle or solve. We must work together to consciously and subconsciously solve these issues. Part of what we need to learn is how to work together—as One. The point of this entire exercise is that we *are* One, so we must learn to act as one cohesive unit. All mankind is One. One with each other and One with God.

It's the most important lesson we are here to learn.

With the help of you and many others, God's plan is to raise the planet's shared consciousness to a new level, never known before. A level where we all can experience the glory of an earthly life well before we ascend to the Heavens and someday to another solar system (an alternate Universe).

It will be much the same as this one—a playground for our enjoyment and eventual growth. This is a repeating pattern in the Universe. One that mankind is not yet aware of. With your help and that of our other Ascended Masters though, someday all mankind will know and experience this type of monumental growth.

Lesson 2 - God's Plan

God has a plan unknown to most of mankind.

A plan in which He will lift up man to new heights, new teachings, but only if they search and try for answers. They must ASK. It's the key. No asking, then no spurring onto new thoughts, new resources and new advancements.

We all have this capability, but few try and therefore few take advantage of it.

We all should know by now that there is more to life than what we experience. We can feel or sense things, but we must pay attention. We must be aware. Aware of ourselves, our own body, and the world around us.

One who pays attention can see his relationship with the outside world. One who does not open his eyes to this reality will remain stuck to the old ways.

Those who can see, need to be the light (or the eyes, as it were) for the others—those individuals blind to outside occurrences.

It's imperative we help each other, lift each other up, light the way to move mankind forward.

This is done in a myriad of ways.

Encouragement is one such way. It is a kind and loving method used to spur another to greatness, to help them be all they can be. It's the mastery of the method of encouragement that will lead this planet forward. We must all do our part.

Another method is **Empathy.** We must learn to exhibit empathy for the plight or path of others. Not judging, for that alone is reserved for God and even then, God's only requirement is that we each try our very best, without limits, for then we know (and God knows), our best effort was given.

There are no regrets if you give your best and come in second or last. You know in your heart you have done the best to your ability.

Back to empathy. The kindness and sorrow we feel for others are important to comprehend. No man will advance if he cannot feel the pain and sorrow of another.

Remember we are all connected.

To deny the feelings of another is to deny yourself a part of yourself. This is not what God wants; He prefers we treat each other with kindness as if it was us with whatever affliction, because it truly is us, a part of us, with the here-to-for-mentioned affliction. Important lesson to learn.

Another trait we are to accept is the practice of **Gratitude-**giving. This doesn't have to be a daily list, although that practice will help many develop the habit, but rather a continuous appreciation for all one has, is capable of, and for the wonderment of our beautiful planet.

Living a grateful life is an on-going state of being, not something to complete merely because it's on your "to do" list.

It's truly a way of being, something that permeates through one's body, that comes straight from the core of a grateful heart.

Lesson 2 - God's Plan

Lesson 3 - Playgrounds

The world continues to be a playground for mankind to learn lessons and it will be so until such time as all become kindred spirits leading towards Ascension.

When all have learned all the lessons, they will ascend to the heavens above and God will destroy their beautiful home, the Earth. It will exist no more.

All beings, upon their turns, will eventually ascend to another, even better/brighter solar system, where God will again prepare a wonderful playground for their enjoyment and growth. This new place will be called Taos—New World.

Beings will appear (look) differently, without so many features, for they will have learned that physical features do not define a person. It will be the heart or the spirit or even the soul inside each of us that will be the pertinent part of our beings. This is easier to accept once we have learned these lessons: outside or exterior ≠ the interior. We all should delve to understand the "interior" of others if we are to learn these lessons and advance or ascend to the next level.

Future lessons to learn involve acting with even more compassion and love to others at a level that even the most advanced beings at present cannot comprehend. Yes, there is much more to learn and there will continue to be so.

Mankind or extraterrestrial beings as we really are, actually have many more lessons to learn. This will take eons to discover, learn and absorb into our souls.

Lesson 4 - **The Process**

We all have things we don't know or understand. Being on this journey helps us to find these answers. All we have to do is ASK. The answers will come in the most serendipitous ways. It will seem like happenstance, but it is all carefully planned out by God Himself, as much as our life is planned.

We all have free will to do as we choose, but the lessons we are here to learn are all set in stone before we are to arrive.

You see, how are we to learn and grow if we do not learn the lessons? Yes, lessons can be painful, yet we should be thankful, for without the lesson there is no growth, there is no change. Learn to accept these challenges or experiences as a part of life. It's part of living your best life.

Failure to learn means one merely has to repeat the lesson. Reason it is so important to pay attention.

We all can do better in life, but in order to do better, we must know better. To know better, we must learn and grow. Experiences or challenges on Earth is the way God teaches us these lessons. This is the reason being allowed to experience life on Earth is such a cherished experience.

Hard learners, or students most interested in advancing, are chosen first and then allowed repeat experiences. It's quite a competitive or shall we say a "sought-after" experience.

When one's time comes to advance to an earthly visit, proper preparations are made. The memory is wiped clean, except for some of the lessons. Reason is to avoid confusion of past lives. You wouldn't want to be living an experience or life in one time and culture and become confused with an earlier situation.

However, strong connections with some people, your clan, or connectors, is still maintained through feelings. You are able to feel some sort of connection. This feeling transcends lifetime experiences. Reason that as we advance and become more in touch with our feelings, we will experience a "knowing" or sense of ease when we first encounter one of these beings.

Such is the case for Soulmates and even more so for Twin Flames. The connection is so strong, one cannot ignore it. One might not understand it at the time, but nevertheless, it cannot be ignored.

Lesson 5 - The Cornerstones

Kindness, Faith, Love and Trust are the cornerstones for building a good life.

Man needs all four to lead a productive and essential life.

<u>Kindness</u> teaches us about others. When we are self-centered and self-serving, and not showing or feeling kindness to others we will not thrive or grow.

Kindness teaches us many lessons, one of which is to put the well-being of another or others before ourselves. The miracle is that by doing so, we actually help ourselves. We grow. We learn to be compassionate towards others. We treat others as God would want. And it fills a need deep inside our souls. A need we cannot understand or fathom until we experience it.

<u>Faith</u> is another necessary component, one that will carry us a long way. A long way as in over a long period of time, but also a long way in the sense of soothing or comforting our souls. In times of need and despair, it will carry us through. The lesson learned, among others, is that by having Faith in God and His ways, we will be carried through our trauma (or opportunity for growth, as we often refer to such challenges).

Do not be afraid to ask God for help and accept His help. This is part of the process of Faith. It also feeds and soothes our inner soul.

Love is by far the most important, the deepest and longest-lasting feeling we are here on Earth to experience. To experience a life of deep and abiding love is to experience one, if not the most, deeply divine experiences on Earth. The love stays in your heart through multiple lifetimes. You may not always understand it, but you will always feel it.

The most advanced masters are so filled with love that it encompasses their whole or entire being.

Love is where the "light" comes from. Those advanced in feeling love as a continuous way of life put off a glow—a light—that others can almost see. In fact some *can* see it. Nonetheless, others can certainly feel it.

This light inspires others even if they aren't aware of what is happening. They will tend to follow or be drawn to others "with the light." This is how they will learn and grow. Reason it's important to always set a good example...others tend to always observe. If they "catch you" doing good, it spurs something inside of them to do the same. They aren't even always aware of this as it can be their subconscious leading them.

Trust is also a necessary component for one's development and growth. We all must learn to trust God for He and only He has complete control over our Universe. We control our growth (or lack thereof) but He controls the classroom, as it were.

The way to build Trust is to have it. The way to have it, is to Trust. It's a never-ending circle or cycle. You just have to jump in like a merry-go-round. Start wherever you are and take that leap of faith.

Trust has a way to calm our inner souls. If we Trust in God, we feel a calmness not experienced in other ways. It's necessary to get to this place of calmness in order for us to grow.

When we are calm, we are kinder to others. It also helps to maintain or attain the proper vibrations for our lives to work perfectly together. Trust helps get you there.

Once you learn to Trust in God, your life begins to "flow." This is the Heavenly Flow of Life that God wishes for all mankind. One of the important lessons we are all here to learn.

Peace and Joy follow when one learns to Trust. Trust is also linked to Love. Greater Love can be received if we Trust it will come in God's timing.

Lesson 5 - The Cornerstones

Lesson 6 ⋅ The Game of Life

More lessons to learn my friends.

We all must be open—open with our hearts and souls and conscious and unconscious minds in order to receive these many lessons.

First and foremost is our treatment of self and others.

We must be kind to ourselves like we are, or should be, to others. Our unconscious mind becomes our conscious mind, which becomes our reality. It is important to feed it good thoughts, happy thoughts, thoughts of things we love and desire, for it will eventually become manifested as a physicality. So very important.

Many people do this incorrectly and therefore manifest the very thing or things they do *not* want! Be careful. Be aware. Wish and dream wisely. Be kind to yourself. Only say nice and loving things in your mind to yourself. Think well of yourself. Believe you are worth it, for you *are* worth it in the eyes of God.

We are all worthy of greatness and a loving life full of happiness and joy and friendship and beautiful surroundings. We all can do it, but it starts in the subconscious.

Like this:

Subconscious Thoughts (Manifestation) ➔
Conscious Thoughts ➔ *Your Reality*

It's really just that simple. Once one knows and practices this, life is a brand-new game. One in which we are all winners. How glorious is that? Reason God knows all and can perfect the "Game of Life" so well.

Remember, Earth is merely a playground for our learning and growth.

Another lesson is kindness to others and the well treatment of them. Since we are all connected, to be unkind is like being mean or unjust to a part of yourself. Think of it as part of your own body. If your leg hurt, you would tend to it, correct? You would cover it in bandages, wash it and be careful with it. You would nurture it until it mended in God's timing.

Do the same for your dear friends and even others you may not know well, for we are all God's children. Tend to them with loving care; help them when needed, nurture them; give proper medicines or herbs, whatever it takes. Listen to them; guide them and support them. Encourage them. Pay money for their wellness.

It's all part of caring for each other... another part of ourselves, our very own being, as it were.

We are All connected.

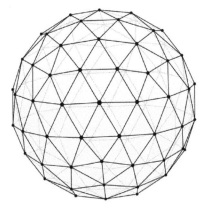

See: we are all part of the same orb, the same cohesive unit.

Image copyright microone via 123rf.com

[Editor's Note: This concept came as an image. Each dot represents one of us.]

If we don't learn to treat ourselves and others with kindness, we cannot advance to other levels of growth. We will remain stuck in agony and discontent, looking to others as "scapegoats" or the reason for our meager existence.

This is so very important for the advancement of mankind.

Lesson 6 - The Game of Life

Lesson 7 · Just Ask

When mankind is weary and cold, let God be what warms him and keeps him safe.

This is quite easy, but one must be knowledgeable about how it is done.

One must ask for comfort and caring. One must ask to feel loved by the Heavenly Father. We all are already loved, all the time, however we might not be in tune enough to feel it. Just ask to feel loved and it will come—the feelings of hopelessness will fade away and hope will return. The feeling of guilt will fade away and be replaced with peace and calm. Feelings of unhappiness will be replaced with faith.

All one needs to do is ASK. Now isn't that an easy and glorious way to live?

All your worries, all your cares, can be easily lifted off your shoulders at any given time. Once mankind learns to accept this process and actually follows through with it, life becomes much more joyous, much fuller, much more complete.

This is how God would have us live. This is how God desires us to live—a joyous, happy, and loving existence. This is one of the miracles we possess by having God the Almighty as our gentle and loving creator.

Do not let this miracle pass you by. It is a miracle to be absorbed, to be used in time of need, and to be used often.

Think of this: if you knew you could have, be, or do anything, would you dare to? Well, why not? Afraid of hurt, pain and disappointment?

If so, do you know you can ask God should any of those unfortunate consequences or events occur? Yes! Then lift your worries high to God. Dream big and set high goals, as they should not be squished, for you can do anything with God's help. Any troubles, challenges, or negative feelings can be corrected or dissolved with His aid.

New heights can be achieved. New heights *will be* achieved. It's something we are here to learn. We must learn to Trust God, for He truly has our best interests at heart.

Lesson 8 - Trust and Calmness

More on trust and how it works.

First, we must step out in blind faith, uncertain if we will receive what we request. But be patient and wait.

In God's perfect timing, all will be known. All will come to fruition. All will be as He and you desire. Just trust.

Whether it be money, love, relationships, babies, a home or precious food, all comes to those who ask for God's grace and wait for completion. The answers may not look like what you expected, but they will come, nonetheless.

Patience is truly a virtue we must all strive to learn. Very important. Being in a rush or demanding does not work well with God (or even with others).

Part of the reason is our vibrations. When we are hurried and rushed, we are not in the correct vibration of the Universe or God's vibration, as it were. We are in the wrong frequency. He can hear us (as always), but we are unable to hear or communicate with Him.

This is the reason being relaxed and in a state of calm is so helpful for maintaining the correct vibrations. Reason we all need to be calmer and more loving. This state of peace leads to settling on the right vibrations. We must learn how to do this— get in the right vibrational mode and maintain it—if we are to be in control of our lives and capable of seeking and knowing full truth and happiness. This is how the Masters among us do it.

You don't see the exceptional beings yelling and screaming and turning red in their face. No, instead you see a smiling, gentle face, with kind eyes and a hopeful demeanor who tries to guide others (gently) to new ways. You must learn to do the latter if we are to raise the consciousness of the planet.

Someday, interactions among humans will all be in the second scenario. Once that is accomplished, all the kindred souls will advance to the heavens and our work here will be done or completed.

How long it takes will be dependent on our cohesive efforts, if we ask for God's help, and if we truly desire to learn and grow. It is each individual's responsibility to aid in the joint development of our cohesive unit, for all will not advance to the new world order until the very last being has accepted this way of life, this way of being.

You see, at the next level, there will be so much more to learn that the short time on Earth will only be a "practice" for the next life on our journey. Just a tiny blip on the timeline of existence, but a very important blip, nonetheless.

Think about these words and act as if they are true:

Have trust.

Have patience.

And strive to do as God has instructed.

All He requires is your best efforts.

Lesson 8 - Trust and Calmness

Lesson 9 - Trust and Truth

We are also to learn about Trust and Truth and how and why they are so very important.

With Trust it is trusting the unknown. With Truth, it is also unknown. Sounds unusual, right? The reason is, we don't always know the Truth. We think we know the Truth, but sometimes we only know part of the story.

Think of the man who steals a loaf of bread. Society (the police, the shop owner, and others) think he's a bad person. They think he's evil. They call him names. They chastise him. They make fun of him. They are generally mean and unloving to him.

They do not know he has an invalid child at home. His wife, whom he loved and adored, has died in some tragic accident. His child has no food. He has no job at the present, but he has been a hard worker, although a lower-class worker all of his life.

They have only a few items at home that can be eaten. The cupboards are literally bare. He does have a small part of a jar of peanut butter, but it is not sufficient for the both of them. He would give it all to the child, but he knows he must look for work or they both will perish.

A loaf of day-old bread from the table outside the shop is the only way he knows to make a palatable meal, so they both can survive.

God has promised him his situation will change. Perhaps he's even been instructed by God to take the small loaf of day-old bread that others would only buy to feed ducks at the park.

He's hesitant. He's scared. He doesn't want to take the bread. He's never done a dishonest thing in his life. But the will to survive and provide for his son is overwhelming, so he takes the bread.

Now that you know the whole story, the situation is quite different. This is how life is. We seldom know the whole or complete story. Humans tend to judge without knowing all the facts. They tend to be mean and unkind in their judging of others. Reason judging is reserved for God and God alone.

We need to remember not to judge others. We must remember we don't know all the facts, or the whole and complete story. We need to remember to give others the benefit of the doubt for we never know the struggles they are experiencing.

Their troubles may be great or their troubles may be few. It's not up to us to judge whether their troubles are sufficient to garner a certain action.

We should remember to treat all with kindness and grace. Help them when we can. Lift them up, not push them down.

Such is the action desired by God. Such is our duty to God and ourselves if we are to grow, which is the purpose we are here.

Next time we observe such an action or even hear of it—remember we do not know the whole story. Remember it is not our job to judge. Remember to think of the person's position and be kind in your thoughts.

This is how we will learn the real truth, by trusting there is more to the story than we observe with our eyes or hear with our ears.

Lesson 9 - Trust and Truth

Lesson 10 · Complacency

We must also learn not to be complacent.

To be complacent in times of need (of others) is the same as aiding in their detriment.

God does not want us to "turn a blind eye." If we see injustice—if we hear injustice—we are to help when and where we can. Lift others up. Help with money. Help with time. Help with your special gifts, whatever they may be. We all have something we can offer or do.

Look at these situations as an opportunity for growth, not merely as an inconvenience in your daily life of collecting or spending more money on things.

These little acts of kindness do not go unnoticed. They do not go unseen. God sees and notices your every effort, no matter how small.

Your inner soul grows more God-like when you reach out to help others. The miracle of helping others is that it will actually help *you*.

Think of that—by helping others, you are actually helping yourself. You're helping yourself learn and grow and therefore it leads you or keeps you on the path of Ascension.

Remember, small deeds *do* matter. Take small steps to help others, even if you think it will hardly matter. It matters to those you help. It matters to God.

Lesson 10 - Complacency

Lesson 11 - Trusting God

We shall learn about trusting God today.

All mankind has issues to cure, which is the reason he/she are here on their journey. Their issues require they learn lessons, often uncomfortable lessons. This is the reason they must learn to trust God, for God knows what is best for them and all creatures or beings.

Give your life over to God and you'll have a happy and productive life. You will learn the many lessons you were sent here to learn.

This is the reason most men do *not* learn the lessons. They are not willing to turn over their life to God; they want to control every outcome, every desire.

Turning over your life to God is not only more efficient, it is the proper thing to do in God's eyes.

This doesn't mean one sits and waits their entire life. It simply means you let go of the outcome or the results.

You have your dreams. You strive towards them, doing the very best to your ability, using your brain and other senses such as intuition to guide you, to lead you. You elicit help or assistance from other learned beings. You do your very best. You work hard. You work diligently. You develop the habit, which is so very necessary for success.

Remember: *Focus + Habit* → *Success/Results*

The key difference is: *you let go of the results*, for only God is in control of the results. How and why He does this is of no consequence to you. Suffice it to say, the results will be in your best interest, even if it may not seem so at the time. All will be known later, someday.

Keep these knowings [Editor's Note: They used this word to indicate a feeling that you know something to be true.] in mind as you go through your life for a happier, more productive, and calmer existence here on Earth—for this is how it all works or operates in the eyes of God.

Adapting such a belief will carry one far in the ways of acceptance. Acceptance for the ways of God and the Universe.

You see, there is much we don't know about how the Universe actually works on a day-to-day basis.

Lesson 12 ⋅ Trust and Patience

Another scenario that humans need to understand and adopt as their own, is the ability of others to know and advance closer to God.

They need not be jealous.

They need not be envious.

They just need to wait their turns.

They need to continue to *ask* for knowledge.

Ask for the Holy Spirit to envelop them. Ask for *guidance*. Do their part to seek knowledge and seek understanding. In God's timing, such knowledge will come forward.

It all happens in God's timing, not theirs. Perhaps they need to develop further, *learn more lessons,* or have more experiences before they will advance to the next level of consciousness.

One must be patient for this to occur. Rushing things along *your* timeline doesn't work. We must remain open and loving to whatever God has planned for us. For then, and only then, will great wisdom become known.

One of the keys is to remain "open" to God's knowledge. It will come when the timing is right. Right for you and right for mankind.

Lesson 12 - Trust and Patience

Lesson 13 - Our Missions

We are all here to seek our missions.

If we are aware and awake and diligent in our efforts and the timing is right in God's way, the missions will be completed. If not, the mission will wait until the next lifetime, or the next class, as it were.

Do not rush.

Do not worry.

Remember life is a journey.

Just do your best each time, each visit, for *that* is all God requires.

Few among us can grasp such a lesson or mission on only one visit, like the great Jesus Christ. Reason he is so revered by us and by God. He was one of God's many miracles. The closest thing to His son.

His creation made or created for a great and wondrous purpose as those who seek knowledge—and study Jesus— have found.

In other religions there is a similar occurrence to show God or their God's great magnificence and to lead others to the Divine. This miracle is not reserved for Christianity alone. It just takes other forms in the other religions. This will be explained later in more detail.

All that is asked at this time is that mankind remain with an open heart and open mind to the endless possibilities created by God in our Universe.

In the end, all will be known.

All beings will understand, for it is a requirement of lifting off to our next level of consciousness.

Lesson 14 - Levels of Consciousness

The next level of consciousness.

Yes, there are many, many levels—in the event that one is curious and wonders about such things.

Not only does man progress with each lifetime here on Earth, someday when all kindred spirits have learned the many lessons we are here on Earth to learn, we will all ascend as One to a new, better, and brighter Universe to again learn new and more lessons in a playground created by God.

These many lessons will again take years—eons and eons—in the current understanding of mankind about time. These lessons will be deep, much deeper than the current mankind is capable of understanding.

But we will eventually gain all the understanding that God desires for us. Once again, all will ascend to the Heavens. All will ascend to above, and our beautiful and great playground, created solely for our entertainment and learning, will cease to exist.

This will not be a time of sadness as one might expect. It will be the same here on Earth once we are ready to advance.

It will be joyous.

A time to celebrate.

A time to be ever so thankful to our dear God above for teaching us so we may grow.

We will all be proud in our souls for what we have accomplished. We will know we did our very best and finally achieve what God planned for us.

Peace and Joy will fill our hearts and souls. It will be an extremely happy time in our everlasting existence.

You see, we really will exist forever. Yes, FOREVER!

We are all made of energy. Energy never dies, it is just transformed to another dimension or condition. (The word cannot be exactly translated at this time in human development. More or better descriptions to be given later.)

Nonetheless, as we are created from energy by our great Heavenly Father, we will never cease to exist. We will merely be transformed to something better and brighter during each iteration.

This is a glorious miracle to behold.

It is one of the many plans of God, set in stone, oh so long ago. So long ago that we cannot even fathom the time with the feeble minds we now have—and we know our minds are not actually feeble as they are quite capable of many things. It's merely the comparison that many make in our current state of consciousness and intellectual capabilities that we may *seem* feeble. This is not a put-down, but merely a way to show comparison in terms humans can understand at the present time.

On to another lesson.

Lesson 15 - Duality

Man is here to learn many lessons, the least of which is to love one another.

These lessons are deep and often painful. Do you ever wonder why it is so painful? Why it hurts so within your heart and sometimes even within your soul, to lose a special loved one?

It is because it's a lesson to us. It's to show us what we've lost, what is no longer available to us in human, physical terms.

For if we always had the love, we would come to expect it, to take it for granted. By losing it we come to appreciate and value what we lost.

This is the process of Duality and one example of the way it works here on Earth and why it is part of our existence on Earth. Many things will be seemingly "taken" from us while on our journeys, but this is merely to teach us lessons that we would not otherwise learn. Without Duality, there would be no advancement.

Think about it—if your life were already "perfect" — what would there be to learn?

What incentive would there be to grow?

What would even be the purpose of our existence?

Therefore, God created Duality for the lessons to be clear. With the dichotomy of experiencing "having" and "not having," the picture becomes much clearer.

Lesson 16 - Happiness

Another day, another lesson.

Today we'll learn about Happiness—why it's important and why we should strive for it.

Remember back when you were a child? You were happy and carefree. If your early life were as God wanted, that's how your days would be.

Wouldn't it be nice to have every day be carefree and without worries? Playing outside. Running. Chasing friends. Laughing. No worries. Only fun times.

That is what God wants us to have as adults. It's our job or mission to figure out how to make it so.

The way is by planning, structuring our day to move ahead in the proper ways so we learn and grow. We advance. We take care of our own basic human needs. Perhaps we have a family. Perhaps we start our mission at a young age. At any rate, we learn and grow and hopefully learn how to be happy within ourselves.

We learn (or should learn) that Happiness is found within ourselves, not another. No one else can bring you Happiness.

It's not like an apple or piece of meat — a tangible thing — although it feels just as "real." No, Happiness is found within us—deep, deep within some damaged souls. So deep they feel it's not even there. So deep they think it's lost, or they were left out when Happiness was distributed to all. Nonetheless, it *is* there.

It's our job to find it. Use it and bring Happiness to others.

No, you don't give Happiness to others, as I've just said. Happiness can't be obtained from others.

Instead, you *exhibit* Happiness through your kind words and actions. A smile. A cheerful hello. By keeping Happiness as your mainstay, your normal state of being, others will notice. It will spur them to seek Happiness.

Share your joy with others, but not in a way of the braggart, but in a joyous, happy way. Others will be drawn to you. They will start to see the joy and happiness in their own life. They will replicate your actions.

These are ways you spread happiness and joy to others so they can learn to be happy within themselves.

You see, humans are very contagious beings. What one has or exhibits is easily spread to another. Wouldn't it be far better to spread joy and happiness instead of fear and hate?

We have the choice—free will—to do so. So, choose wisely, my dears.

How to "feel" Happiness and joy is all a matter of mindset. Get your mind on worry and doubts and that is what you will surely spread to others. Set your mind on killing, hatred, fears, and wars, and that is the mindset you will incite in others.

But if you have a mindset of wonder, joy, contentment, peace, and love then that is what you will spread.

Think carefully about what type of person you wish to be and exhibit those habits, that lifestyle, and it all comes by your own mindset.

What is mindset? (If you don't know.) It's the way you look at the world and everything in it. It's how your mind (your brain) processes your current situation. It's how you look at things, your environment, and your very own life.

Surely there will be times that aren't all rosy, and cheerful. Times of death and destruction and great loss— not just to buildings and things—but great loss of life. Unbearable loss where we think we just cannot go on another day, another hour, or another minute.

In those times it's especially important to maintain a good mindset. One way to do so is to remember these things:

This too shall pass.

It's part of learning a lesson.

God never gives you more than you can handle.

So at these times, it's important to look for Hope. Look for Gratitude and express these thoughts to others.

For example: if your farm and home are destroyed by a tornado, be thankful your family is intact with few injuries; your family dog is still with you (in fact, he's a good example to follow with his wagging tail and wet kisses). Perhaps your grain is still okay. Maybe your water supply is still available.

Whatever your situation, there is undoubtedly something to be thankful for.

And then there's the lesson. The lesson we are to learn.

Perhaps we are to learn that God alone is in control.

Perhaps we are to learn the importance of family over "things."

Perhaps we are to learn we can rebuild, and we have the strength, knowledge, capability, and drive to do so.

Perhaps we are even to learn it is time to move on and make new choices or life decisions after some horrific occurrence.

Whatever and however we decide to move on, it's all a matter of mindset and what type of mindset we decide to adopt.

That mindset will help us to be happy or unhappy.

That mindset will spread like wildfire to others.

Choose your mindset carefully. Choose your mindset with an eye towards happiness, for it IS all within your control, your free will.

Lesson 16 - Happiness

Lesson 17 · Truth

Another area of complexity is Truth.

What is it, really?

What constitutes the Truth? How important is it to tell the Truth? Are we responsible for telling the Truth even when it will hurt others?

Does it justify telling the Truth when we say, "I'm telling you this for your own good?" We think not.

God thinks not.

We must always be kind and loving to others, especially when it comes to areas like the Truth. To crush someone's spirit and soul with unkind words, even if they *are* true, is mean and unthoughtful if done with a spirit of meanness.

Many do this habit regularly and they smirk or smile to themselves at the same time.

They think they are being courageous and enjoy the put-down of others. If makes them feel big to make others feel small. This is a time and manner not to tell the Truth.

There are much kinder, much gentler, and more effective ways to tell the same Truth.

Let us remember how our actions affect others, as we are all connected. To say or do mean things that would naturally elicit hurt and pain in another is to, in effect, hurt ourselves. We don't want to hurt ourselves (unless we have some underlying issues).

Should you ever feel the desire to take hurtful actions in the name of Truth, immediately go to God and ask for your own healing, for you are the one who needs to hear the Truth.

Now, on to other situations where the use of Truth shall be debated.

Remember as a child when your parents (hopefully) told you to always tell the Truth? This was good advice. Did you do it or did you blow their advice away like the air?

If you didn't follow their advice, hopefully there was some sort of consequence, so you learned it was far better to just be Truthful from the beginning.

This is one of the many duties of a parent—to teach and show their children to tell the Truth. They should exhibit what they teach also, for children learn far more by what they "see" versus what their parents "say."

Remember your duties whether you are a parent or a child. The child's role/part is to listen to their parents and obey their instructions. Learn these Truths as it were, to tell the Truth and not lie, so they can also lead a more exemplary life.

Such is as God wishes for all of us eternal beings. The longer we fail to learn this lesson, the longer we will suffer, both individually and as a cohesive unit.

Think about this often: when to tell a lie or when to tell the Truth. The wise among us will certainly learn it is always important to be Truthful. The choice is how to deliver the news...with brutal hurtful honesty that scares the soul and diminishes one's spirit, or with hope and love that such instruction will lead another to a more positive result.

The choice is ours. God has merely prepared the lesson.

On to another topic.

Lesson 18 - Hope and Love

Hope and Love go together.

This might seem like an odd pair, but we will explain.

When we are filled with Hope, we are happy and joyful inside because we are looking forward to the future.

It is much the same with Love. We are happy and joyful inside, sometimes all the way into our souls. We are happy today and we believe we will be happy in the future.

But that is not always the case with Love. Sometimes we become upset, mad, or perhaps even crushed by the actions of another and our Love may turn to hate or grief or even ambivalence.

Love can transform to another feeling. Later it might return to Love, but it is surely transformed depending on our thoughts and feelings.

What if *you* could control your thoughts of Love and feel Love all the time, like one does with Hope each new day?

We can! It's a matter of mindset.

When the actions of another seem to turn your Love for them to some other emotion try this: separate their actions from them.

You can still love them, but not their actions. You don't have to accept their poor actions, just separate it from them. This helps you maintain your Love for them.

For you see, others can feel our Love for them even if it is not expressed. They can feel when your Love turns to hate, disdain, or disappointment.

This does not spur good actions on their part. In fact, it does quite the opposite—it spurs them to continue down the wrong path, a path without Hope, without Love. In a way, it contributes to their continued poor choices and even poorer actions.

Think about this: if you felt no one loved you and no one cared, mighten you do some unlawful or unkind act?

"What's the point?" you might surmise, "As no one cares anyway."

The thoughts, the prayers, the caring and the love can be felt by all of us even if we are not aware of it.

The reason is clear—we are all One.

Lesson 19 ⸱ Gratitude

The lesson today has to do with Gratitude and why it's so very important as a method to bring us closer to God.

Think about it. If we had everything we could want or need all the time; would we be grateful? Probably not, because we'd expect it.

When something is "there" or with us always, it is what we expect. We know nothing different. It is always so.

But when something is lacking, or is taken away from us, well, that is quite a different story. We seem helpless without it. We cry. We shout out to God, "Why did you take 'it' from us?"

We are inconsolable. We are sad. Our inner soul is broken, or so it feels. We are in the depths of despair.

All this feeling of "without" is only possible when we no longer have the cherished item. Would it even be cherished if it were not taken from us? Probably not, because we would just expect it to be always there or here with us.

Such is the lesson that God teaches.

For we will never acknowledge the value, the goodness, the need or however much we love someone or something, until we no longer have it.

God uses this method to help us appreciate all the wonderful things and people he gives us or brings into our lives. Without this dichotomy or duality, we would never experience the "without" or the loss, the deep, deep loss of something dear to us.

This is how one learns to be Grateful.

Grateful for all we do have and grateful to God for teaching us to be Grateful for what we have and experience in our life here on Earth.

For if we never experience this duality, we would remain spoiled children and never grow into the higher beings that God desires for us.

He delights in our growth, much like a parent when their little child finally grasps something new. It's not that God wants to hurt us, but he knows learning a lesson has a cost—a price—as it were. Pain, hurt and emotional turmoil and even physical pain, is sometimes the price we must pay to learn the lesson.

Do not lash out at God during these lessons, although it may seem quite necessary to do so. Be accepting of these lessons for they will make you grow and learn the ways of God.

After learning the lessons, you will become more God-like. You will have greater understanding. You will grow into your Higher Self.

This growth, however painful, *is* quite necessary for the Ascension of Mankind, which is God's goal for our planet at this time and it should be your goal (even if you aren't aware of it quite yet) and it should be the goal of all mankind.

Your part, and the part of others, is quite important in the mission of lifting up the world. We all must do our part as this is a long and tedious journey.

If we all work together, as One, it will be a smoother journey. We can help each other accept the ways or wishes, as it were, of God. We can make the journey a little less painful. We can help each other understand why and appreciate the good in our lives.

By working together, the journey can be more efficient, more direct, and not so circuitous (round about). This is what God desires, for we are all One—one cohesive unit, one co-mingled soul, experiencing life here on Earth at this time together.

We are One.

The continuing lesson. The most important lesson we are here to learn.

Lesson 19 · Gratitude

Lesson 20 · Favoritism

The next lesson is on Favoritism.

It may seem like God has favorites—those who seem to be happy and receive all the earthly things they desire or need.

However, one only sees or understands part of the story. There are many reasons for this so-called perfection in others.

Let us explain two of them.

In one instance a person has seemingly all that he needs or could want; however, one day it will all change and the most important things to them will be taken in a flash.

It could be their family, their health, their wealth or perhaps a physical impairment will occur. They will be in despair. They will be on a rapid learning curve to experience the duality of being "without."

They will learn to be ever so grateful for what they previously had and for what seemingly little they now have. They will learn. They will grow.

Now to the other instance, the other scenario. One seems perfectly content and has all they would need, seemingly a "perfect" life to others looking in at them in observance.

However, this is not the case at all. These people have already been through their own trials and tribulations. They have learned to accept God's will, God's timing and God's lessons with an open heart or a heart of Gratitude for whatever God bestows on them and their family.

All seems perfect, but the storms have passed, and new storms are dealt with in a different manner—a positive and accepting manner.

A manner of Gratefulness and Love.

You see, the journey or path of others is their journey alone, not our journey. Some similarities exist, certainly, which do help us with kindness, understanding, and relatability for other's trials, but remember we *all* have our own journey.

So when you see another, it is not for you to judge —"Oh, they have an easy journey and mine is much more difficult."

No, it's God's job to decide the lessons one is to learn and the methods, hence the difficulty of the journey.

We all have free will and sometimes one's free will makes the journey harder or easier (seemingly) but that is a more complicated lesson to be dealt with later.

Suffice it to say we are all on our own journey to learn great lessons. Gratitude is one such great lesson to learn.

We are not here to judge the difficulty of another's lesson or compare them to ourselves. Our job is to learn *our* lessons and help others cope and learn their lessons. No judging on our parts. If another is slow to learn we can relate what we've learned; we can encourage them; we can show or explain how to be grateful.

This is all so very important to do because remember:

We Are All One.

One cohesive unit.

Lesson 20 ⁄ Favoritism

Lesson 21 · Acceptance

Be authentic—to others and to yourself.

This means to not deny your natural self. You are a loving being with feelings, desires, and dreams.

That's how you are meant to be here on Earth. It's part of the journey to accept how you are, in the state of being which God has created you.

This means to accept *all* of you, complete with the flaws, the marks of imperfection and all.

Ever wonder why somewhat unsightly marks on the body are called "beauty marks" when they may seem unsightly? It's because we must learn to see and accept our imperfections as a sign of beauty or something that makes us special.

We all have something to make us special. Learning to discover it and accept it is one of the lessons we are here to learn.

An easy example to understand is the outer physical layer. We have curly hair, yet we desire straight. We want *some* hair, yet we are bald. We want tattoos, yet we have none (so we add them).

We lament we aren't tall enough or we are too chubby; we are too slow to run, or our teeth are crooked.

Certainly, it is our free will to change those physical characteristics we feel we must, although it is not necessary.

If it is doable and makes us feel better, then certainly proceed with the "improvements," but the deeper meaning is learning self-acceptance. Acceptance for all you are and all you can be.

Your outer beauty does not equal your inner beauty.

Once we become comfortable with ourselves, we are next to learn not to be so judgmental of the outer beauty of *others*.

You see, as we grow, we change. We may or may not like the changes. We have to learn to accept ourselves and our outer beauty at all the stages of life. Almost as if we are different people, albeit someone we already knew. Because we are constantly evolving, hopefully. This is part of what we are here to learn.

Accepting others is part of the process too. Don't be quick to judge one's outer beauty or lack thereof.

The important part of all of us lies within. Learn to accept that part as well. This lesson will serve mankind well on our continuous journey.

On to beauty.

Beauty is truly in the eye of the beholder! Ever see a man truly mesmerized with a woman whom others may consider unattractive or even ugly? Yes—he sees something quite different.

Ever see a seemingly beautiful woman and yet some men are not the least bit attracted? It's like that.

Some people see beauty one way and others see it quite differently. It's not for us to judge their likes or dislikes, but merely to observe and differentiate the desires of others.

One way to do so is to learn not to be judgmental of other's outer beauty. Accept all just as they are, the same as you wish to be accepted. And hopefully the way you have already learned to accept yourself.

This process may take well into adulthood. It may take lifetimes. It may take until one's very last breath, but it is an understanding well worth the effort to learn.

Lesson 21 ⁄ Acceptance

Lesson 22 - Acknowledgment

The lesson today is about Acknowledgment.

Acknowledgment of God and His place in our great Universe and Acknowledgment of All That Is and will be.

You see, when God created the Earth as we know it, He had a purpose in mind, a grand vision, unknown to mankind.

Over the years, some men and women have searched for answers through religion and other methods. They have cracked the code, as it were, about why we are here and the lessons to learn. Usually these were the "repeat visitors" to Earth, those who frequently are blessed with return visits and learn quickly.

Every once in a while a "newbie" will be so inclined and make great progress, even on one visit.

You are one such being. Multiple trips but not too much progress till this visit. [Editor's Note: They are speaking specifically to the author here.]

Your journey has been a testament to the over-whelming power of Love, but that lesson will be reserved for another day, along with many other lessons about Love, for it is the strongest power known to mankind and beyond.

Back to Acknowledgement.

We all must learn to accept not just the ways of God—the many traits He deems necessary for our joint Ascension to the Heavens—but we must acknowledge His great powers, His plans, and His purpose for all of us.

This Acknowledgment is difficult for many people. They just simply don't understand or don't want to understand. They are truly blind in a sense to the word of God.

They are not wrong or bad. They are merely unenlightened. It is the job of Archangels above and those angels on Earth to teach them, to show them the way. To be their eyes and to speak the truth and encouraging words in small bits, so they will come around and eventually advance.

Remember, we are all connected; we must *ALL* advance.

No man or woman will be left behind when the Great Ascension takes place. We all must do our parts to ensure All are ready and capable of ascending. It's our duty to ourselves, to mankind, and to God.

"Be the light so others may follow" is one of God's tenants.

We can all do our part to encourage others and lead the way for them.

It starts with believing ourselves, after searching and finding our own answers. Then setting an example for others. Later by speaking words of encouragement. Checking back periodically helps sustain the momentum too. For you never know if you are the only one encouraging another. You could be the sole reason, or you could be the catalyst for their development.

Never underestimate the power of One (meaning just one person) and at the same time, the power of One (all of us).

Quite magnificent—our individual power and joint power. That too will be a lesson for another day.

Suffice it to say, the journey begins with Acknowledgment of God and All That Is, along with God's great plan for us.

How we start the journey is up to us and others who set the stage by their actions and encouragement. However it starts, it's a path we will all learn to take as we make the necessary advancements of mankind and ascend to the Heavens as God has planned for all of us.

Lesson 22 - Acknowledgment

*Lesson 23 - **Memories***

Our next lesson is about Memory.

And how it works with multiple lifetimes that we as beings are fortunate enough to live here on Earth in order to experience the growth necessary for our Ascension.

As we prepare for a return visit to Earth, the great leaders erase or cleanse our Memories. This helps us to function in our new lives without confusion of past lives—the location, the families, the social norms, etc.

Sometimes the Memories are so very strong that even the most advanced cleansing methods are insufficient to clear every Memory.

Such is the case for those who recall past lives.

Certainly, some may be imposters, but most are not. Think about it—why would someone make up such a story only to subject themselves to ridicule and doubt?

As for children, well, they are open books. They will pass along these Memories, these knowings, without even being aware it was an earlier life, for the Memory is so strongly embedded.

It is the same for special soulmates, like yourself. [Editor's Note: They are speaking specifically to the author here.]

In at least one partner there will remain just a glimmer or two of a past life together. Both however, will have a sense of already knowing each other, which they are unable to explain at first. But they feel it, nonetheless.

This is part of God's plan to bring them together for a great purpose. For they will have an important assignment necessary for the advancement of mankind. By feeling so attached, so close to another being, it spurs their growth—both as a human and as a spiritual leader for others. It's all part of God's plan.

Let these words sink in, for they are very powerful.

Let not naysayers sway your beliefs, for if you are to ascend to the Heavens as God desires, you will need to accept them to the core of your being.

Lesson 24 - Attitude

Attitude is very important for our growth.

We may not think so, but it is. The way we look at life affects our very life.

It creates our reality.

One may have heard this before, and not paid attention to the saying, but it is indeed true.

You see, it all starts in one's subconscious. Feed it negative and poor thoughts and so your life becomes filled with strife and worry.

Feed your mind positive, uplifting, and good things, and your life will be wonderful.

We must strive to look at the glass as half full, not half empty. This way of looking at life is imperative for our growth if we are to ascend as God plans for us.

You see, those whose life is filled with despair are so worried about their very existence, they can never rise above to tackle more worthy issues.

Think of this, if you are worried for your very existence—the next crust of bread, as it were, to sustain you—you would be hesitant to give it all to God, but that is exactly what one must do to move ahead.

Give your worries to God. Hand them over on a silver plate, so to speak.

Once you do so, your worries are literally given away and you are able to cope with life.

Once you can cope, work on the positive attitude even if things still look bleak.

Your world will start to be brighter. Your interactions with others will improve. You will start to be happier and start to see joy in everyday life.

This is something we all can do and should do at various times during our lives. It is the way God intends for us to live.

There is even more to learn about our attitude and how it affects and shapes our lives. This will be addressed in more detail in future lessons.

Suffice it to say, a good Attitude is a good place to start one's journey with God to a higher form of existence.

Lesson 25 - **Encouragement**

Encouragement is our duty to God, ourselves, and others.

We know now—or should know—how the Encouragement of others can inspire us and spur us to greatness by encouraging and supporting us to accomplish or finish things we only dreamed of but doubted we could accomplish.

Such is Encouragement and it is so important.

With the Encouragement of others, it makes *us* believe we can do so. It raises our attitude. We start to believe we can accomplish such feats. Their words and kind actions reach not only our conscious mind but our subconscious mind.

One can actually spur another to greatness just by their Encouragement.

Think of the little child running a race whose parent is on the sideline, cheering them on. The child will most certainly run faster and try harder with the Encouragement of their parent.

Think of the man trudging to a job every day, a job he may or may not like, but does anyway to support his growing family. When the wife encourages him, infuses him with thanks and gratitude and appreciation and reiterates how she knows he can do this difficult thing, it changes everything. Her words of Encouragement and confidence in his abilities change everything.

He is not only filled with the desire to care for his family, but with the love and respect of his adoring and caring wife. It makes him feel—Yes, he can do anything, and he will do anything to care for his family. He sees his family as the wonderful unit it is and wants to do his part to keep it together. A man will truly do anything for a woman who encourages and supports him.

Greatness is not attained by merely supporting his family in a sustainable method. Great men, well-known men who have impacted mankind through the ages, often have a supportive, caring and encouraging spouse.

The saying, "Behind every great man is a good woman" is certainly true.

The vice versa is true also. Greatness is not only reserved for men. Women who are supported by an encouraging spouse can do great things. They can also make lasting impressions or effect on mankind.

We should all strive to encourage others, not just our families and loved ones.

This is one of the keys to move mankind forward. And it is a painless and easy task to do!

The benefits to be gained are not only on the one receiving the Encouragement, but on us also. For when we give Encouragement to others, it spurs something in us—a feeling of doing good, of accomplishment, of peace, and we then carry this bit of happiness with us.

It's truly a "win/win position" when we encourage others, as the benefits come back to us.

These good feelings also help us, even if subconsciously, as *we* realize we can do the impossible too. By encouraging others, our subconscious is reshaped to our benefit too, raising us to greatness in other ways.

This is a great circle or condition to be in. Very helpful for the Ascension of all mankind.

We should look for opportunities to encourage others daily, for in the end it helps all mankind rise up to the levels God has set for us.

Lesson 25 · Encouragement

Lesson 26 - Fulfillment

Let us talk today about Fulfillment – what it is to you and what it is for others.

When God created the Earth and all the creatures, it was fulfilling a great mission in Him.

He had great plans for all the beings. He was setting things in motion. It helped to fulfill him. It made Him joyous. It made Him proud, and rightly so as it was a stupendous accomplishment!

Our lives are similar to that only not on such a stupendous scale, but similar just the same.

For we are able to create good and magnificent things as well.

We can create whatever we desire. This will fulfill us but only if we create the right things: things that bring us Fulfillment. That is what we are here to learn, along with many other lessons.

We must learn that creating (or manifesting) is well within our power. Then we must learn *what* to create, for man often creates many things that do not bring him joy and Fulfillment before he realizes or learns what does result in Fulfillment.

It is important for all of us to be fulfilled, for it is that filling of our souls with contentment that is the eventual goal, whether we realize it or not.

One may try and try to create what one desires and be very adept at doing so. But unless one creates what will fulfill their soul and lead to contentment within, it will be for naught, as they will continue to feel the loss of something missing.

It is our jobs to seek Fulfillment. It's part of the process here on Earth—part of the reason we are here.

Think of this. The man who creates wealth, seems prosperous as he has all the treasured or seemingly important worldly goods—a nice house, car, and furnishings—yet he feels something is missing. He's created wealth but has no dear and close relationships. He may have a family, but has failed to nurture the relationships so he still feels something is lacking.

In such a situation, he has not yet learned about Fulfillment, only how to manifest and perhaps he is quite good at that. He will need to think or perhaps ask God or his Archangels for suggestions. He will have to dig deep and think about others and what is needed on a grander, wider scale.

Perhaps he will provide some essential items to those less fortunate in another country, like say medicines or eyeglasses or special surgeries. It matters not what it is, but that it is helping others. That is how one becomes fulfilled. That is how one lives a grand and exemplary life.

Each time one's philanthropic efforts are made, others see and others observe. It plants a small seed in them with the notion that they too can do such things, although for a slightly different benefit. His example lights a fire in others, even if it is subconsciously. At some level, his action stirs others to proceed with similar activities.

This is how God intended our world to operate.

We assist each other in our journeys.

We learn lessons along the way. Many lessons to be sure.

We operate as one cohesive unit.

We progress until the very last being has learned how to fulfill themselves, which, along with other lessons, will lead to our eventual Ascension.

Lesson 26 - Fulfillment

Lesson 27 · Sickness and Good Health

Today we learn about Sickness and Good Health.

We have all observed someone or an animal who is sick with some perilous disease or illness.

These afflictions are brought about in a variety of reasons. Most notably from a lack of self-care.

When one does not take proper care of oneself it sends a message to the subconscious, "I am not worthy. I am not important enough to take care of." Such subconscious thoughts often result in the body having some affliction.

The body tells what the soul cannot.

This situation can be easily and quickly corrected.

All one has to do is have a different mindset.

This is accomplished by thinking better thoughts. Better thoughts lead to better actions. Better actions lead to less afflictions or sickness.

Think of this situation: one feels good about themselves, feels worthy of indulging in that special something. It may be a massage or spa day or even quiet time or a movie. It can be indulging in hours on a special hobby.

It doesn't matter the activity. It matters that they feel that they, and their happiness and joy and satisfaction, are important enough to indulge or participate in such an event.

In turn, such action makes them happy and fulfilled. They feel good about themselves. They feel worthy. Therefore, no sickness or death.

They are creating their reality—a happy and fulfilling life. They feel worthy. Sickness is kept at bay because their low feelings and those thoughts of unworthiness do not exist.

Their subconscious mind feeds these thoughts. Reason that self-care is so important. It's often an unsaid way to say, "I'm important; I have value. I deserve this or that."

So many beings do not take this important step and spend their lives living in despair—or without—and feeling unworthy. This is not necessary and easily corrected.

All one must do is ASK.

Ask yourself first of all, "What would I do if I could do anything at this moment—even little things, a little treat?" (Many do not even indulge themselves in the slightest little benefit.)

If you are uncertain how to obtain this little bit of joy—perhaps money or time are limited or guilt to perform other activities is holding you back—just ask God to help you accomplish such a thing.

He is powerful. He can make a way for it to happen even if you cannot fathom how it's done.

Search within for fulfillment and ASK for help when needed.

Your soul needs fulfillment.

One way, or the first way, is to take care of yourself. You are better able to serve others once you have taken care of your own needs. Imperative lesson for us all to learn. We are worth it!

We can do God's work, work we were called to do, but *after* we take care of ourselves. This means self-care and self-love, which we will discuss in detail later in another lesson.

Suffice it to say, it starts with us taking proper care of ourselves. An important lesson indeed.

Lesson 27 · Sickness and Good Health

Lesson 28 - Self-Love

Self-love is an important lesson; one we are all here to learn.

It's important to learn to love ourselves before we can love others. This dynamic is shown numerous times throughout the Bible and other religious teachings.

Love starts with us, to be sure. Then it expands to other beings, other creatures, and the environment.

Eventually love will encompass the Earth.

This is as God desires and a necessary component to mankind's Ascension—something we all must learn.

But how to take those first steps and others leading to Self-love?

It all begins in the subconscious, so we must tell ourselves we are worthy and then follow those thoughts with self-care.

After caring for ourselves and taking care of our needs, we must have Self-love, the act of truly accepting ourselves as we are and loving ourselves despite imperfections. We all have imperfections, or so we think, but God doesn't see our imperfections.

He only sees a being still on their journey, still learning, a "not-quite-finished" entity.

We must learn to accept ourselves as such—imperfect beings, trying our best. Such thoughts will endeavor to make us accept Self-love as a way of life.

This consideration or way of thought is or has been attained by many; but many, many others are still struggling with Self-love and have not really accepted this into their souls.

Many proclaim to love themselves, however their actions show otherwise. They continue poor habits that lead to their destruction and downfalls. They have yet to accept the real meaning of Self-love.

The real, deep meaning is to love yourself wholly, as one with God.

Feel you are worthy.

Feel you are perfect just as you are and how God thinks of you.

Truly, deeply love yourself, so much so that you will do anything for yourself, just as you might for a loved one.

This will bring you peace within. This is not the braggart's way who showers himself with meaningless things. It's the giving to yourself the intangibles that bring the most peace, joy, and contentment—things like quiet time for reflection, a walk in nature, eating nourishing and healthy foods, interactions with animals, and watching the ocean or sunrise/sunset.

Enjoying these little things is a way we consciously or subconsciously show ourselves we are worthy of great things.

We are worthy of such joys, no matter how small they may be or seem at the time. These things lift our spirits and make us happy.

In such a state, we are then able to love *others*.

Very important lesson to learn. More about loving others in another lesson.

Lesson 28 · Self-Love

Lesson 29 · Many Paths to God

Today we learn about finding one's way with God.

This is a very important lesson for all mankind to learn.

It does not matter if one serves God, Buddha, Allah or Spirit, or whatever religion or spiritual belief one adheres to, for the Great One, our Spiritual Leader, is all the same.

You see, the purpose for all religions is to lead one to the same place: a higher, more worthy existence and an eventual Ascension to the Heavens.

Different religions have the same purposes—to lift all mankind—to eventual Ascension.

People are all different, so it follows they need different religions.

In fact, even within religions there are various sects or off-shoots to accommodate the varying belief systems. Many do not even come to the Great One (or God as some may call Him) through religion, having not come across the sect or group that fits or suits them. They join or follow through spirituality which also has many sects or ways. Some follow and believe in fairies. Others believe in Angels.

It matters not the method used.

It matters that the method is followed, and one seeks a path to learning and growing and eventual Ascension.

Along the path we each learn many, many lessons that help with our growth.

We learn through our own life experiences as well as the lessons presented by the various religious groups through their writings or stories handed down through generations. It may be the Holy Bible, or it may be Indian folklore.

It matters not which method, for we are all God's children on our journey, yet we are on a cohesive journey to be experienced by mankind. A very important journey indeed.

For within such a journey or growth experience, mankind would remain stuck in its old ways and not advance morally or grow into higher beings as God wishes. And most undoubtedly, man would not ascend as God desires.

Therefore, God set up this system, a perfect system indeed, where mankind would have many—actually unlimited—choices of connecting to him, so they can learn and grow individually and together.

See how God knows best?

See how God sets everything in place in our wonderful playground, yet gives us free will to discover the best path for us?

For we are each worthy and important beings, truly loved by God. He desired that each of us, all of us, and mankind as a collective unit, ascend to the Heavens.

And someday, it will happen just as God planned.

We must all do our part though, for this magnificent event to occur.

We must work on ourselves, learn our lessons, pay attention to the messages, however they reach us.

We must work with others in our clan and perhaps even those outside our clan (religious group) and urge or encourage them, so we all can make the journey to the next Universe, for no man or woman, however humble, will be left behind.

It is written.

It is God's plan.

You see, we are all One and will therefore ascend as One, with the help and design of God.

When exactly this magnificent happening occurs is determined by mankind's cohesive free will and their actions to make it so.

God is hopeful that the creatures he created and gave all the tools for their advancement will be able to do so within a reasonable amount of time. In human terms, it might not be fathomable, but in terms of the Universe, it is quite possible and eagerly anticipated, for it brings God great joy to see each of us advance and grow.

When you feel that bit of self-satisfaction and proudness within you when you learn something new or do a good deed, that indeed is God inside you. That's His joy that he's sharing with you. He wants you to know what it feels like when you do a good thing. For you see, God is always with each of us.

Lesson 30 - Joy and Happiness

Next lesson is on Joy and Happiness, essential components of our happiness.

We all must experience these feelings, or we will surely incarnate again and again until such feelings are a normal and on-going part of our daily existence, for God wants us to feel joyful and happy all the time, even in times of despair, fear, and unhappiness.

How can this occur at the same time, you ask?

It's very easy actually. Once one has adopted a joyful and happy life, then even strife of an astronomical nature cannot penetrate it and destroy it.

Certainly, those negative or unhappy feelings are felt. They are not to be denied. They are not to be ignored. They are to be felt and experienced.

The difference, however, is those negative feelings do not penetrate one's inner core and remove the Joy and Happiness. Instead, the Joy and Happiness absorbs the bad feelings, understands the bad feelings, learns from the bad feelings, and incorporates it into one's being without destroying us.

We resolve to be stronger and remain happy.

We are thankful for the lesson.

We soften in our negative feelings as we learn the other side, the other side of the coin, as it were.

We open up to other possibilities. We do not let the bad feelings destroy us. Instead we use the experience to expand our awareness and learn.

We become more understanding of others, for that is most likely where those bad feelings are derived from. We learn. We grow. Yet we remain happy and joyful.

This is as God intended.

This is as God desires of us.

This growth and absorption of all feelings, yet remaining happy, will lead us to Ascension and the next steps God has planned for us.

For He has a worthy and great plan set in motion for us here on Earth. It's up to each of us to do our parts—individually and cohesively—to make our journey along this path. The journey that will lead us to Ascension and eventually to new lands.

Lesson 31 · Our Connection to God

God is always with us.

This is an important lesson to acknowledge: there is no separation between God and us.

We are connected always, just like we are connected to everyone and everything. Sometimes this Oneness is difficult to understand.

Let us first explain the comfort of knowing God is always with us.

Just repeating those words, even if one does not believe them at first, will bring a sense of stillness and comfort to the weary. This is because it trains our subconscious to accept these words until we actually *do* believe it.

There is nothing wrong with tricking our minds this way. Actually, this is just part of how our minds work.

Our Subconscious Thoughts →
Our Conscious Thoughts → Reality

Those who truly believe with their heart and soul that God is always with them have a sense of calmness and peace that others usually do not possess. You have observed this phenomenon, no doubt. This is how such souls achieved it. You would desire the same feelings too, no doubt, for it is a joyous way to live.

Upon their encounters with other light beings, their light shines. Others will subconsciously and consciously be in awe of their contentment and desire to have the same.

This is one way the spirit of God is spread to others. We observe in others what we do not have, and in turn desire the same for ourselves.

This observation is reason enough for many to turn to religious teachings. This is a very good thing. We lead by example and then encourage others on the path.

Even this example serves as a mini example of how we are all connected, how our actions affect the thoughts and therefore the actions of others.

This is because we are all connected.

All connected as One.

Our entire Universe, not just the Earth, are connected as One.

We are affected by the tides and the moon. We are affected by activities outside the Earth's perimeter as well...star showers and such. We are all truly One with God, with each other, with animals, with the environment, even with the stars and moon and sun and beyond to the end of the Universe.

Then there is the concept that our Universe does not end, so the process, or "Oneness" as it is called, continues. This is quite a complex thought process and one mankind will not come to fully understand until the next iteration. We are merely planting the seed.

For now, it is important that we come to understand that we are connected in Oneness to God and all things (creatures, beings, and environment) in our Universe.

The actions of one part affects the others.

We all know that weather changes—good or seemingly bad—affect humans and animals. We also know that humans can destroy lands, such as thoughtlessly starting forest fires. This affects the ecosystem and the animals whose homes have been destroyed. We are all connected to our everlasting Universe created by God.

Think about this: when one is unhappy or sad, one goes to God with their worries. After quiet contemplation and perhaps discussion on the matter, one's fears and doubts can be lifted. Such is the power of Oneness.

One might try another tactic if feeling blue—the consolation from a friend, or a loving animal, or perhaps even the ocean or the sunshine. The results will be the same...calmness, a new perspective, and joy will fill our hearts.

Now, do you see how we are all connected?

The miracle of this interconnectedness is part of God's plan. The plan to lead us through many stages of growth and advancement that will take years and years to complete each minor step.

Such is the plan of God and we should endeavor to grow and learn the many lessons along the way. But we should remember that we can call to Him whenever we are in need and He will aid us, for He is always there.

We can and should learn to call on other beings and creatures and the environment too, to seek answers and calm our souls.

This is how God desires, for we are not one man (or one being) on the journey alone.

We are on the journey together.

Together as one cohesive unit, making the journey together.

Let us not forget we have each other for comfort and joy as well as the Great One, God Almighty, whenever, and wherever needed. HE will never leave us—because He simply cannot—since we are all "One."

Lesson 32 - Time

Time is another matter that needs further discussion and explanation.

First of all, time is not a straight line as humans now think.

It's rather a continuum between time and space, more like a timeline. God created this timeline long before the first human arrived at the great planet called Earth.

He set in stone the many lessons we are to learn and they are like markers on the timeline. Only the methods, routes, or paths to those lessons are shaped by mankind through his free will. Since man has free will, when he reaches each marker or lesson is up to him.

God has only set the path in motion.

The exact route we take is up to us. We may take the long way or the most direct way.

That being said, it has ended before it has begun. The past, the future, and even the present have already occurred.

It might not seem so to humans, but this is the case. Part of the reason is that God is all-knowing and has already created our experiences. We are just waiting for them to unfold.

In a way, this should give each of us peace knowing the Great One has already laid out a plan for our life—a wonderful and perfect plan.

This means two things.

First of all, if you don't have what you desire at this moment, there is a reason. If it is part of Gods' plan for example for you to be with a certain loved one, then you will be, but it will be in God's perfect timing, when both of you have learned certain lessons and it is the best time for unification.

If you aren't to be with this certain loved one, there is a reason. Perhaps you are just in each other's life to learn a lesson. God knows the reason and you can uncover the reason too if you dig deep enough or ask your spirit guides for clarification.

So, if all the major points of our lives are already set in stone—beginning to end—then all has already been completed before it has begun, in perfect order. There is, therefore, no reason to fret and worry for we are always exactly where we are supposed to be at any given time.

The hardships have a purpose.

The joys have a purpose.

They are milestones on the pathways of our lives.

One must learn to accept God's timing and the order of things. If we have no control over the order, then what's the point of worrying? Just rejoice in the knowing that our Creator has designed a perfect plan for us.

It depends on how quickly and eager we are to learn the lessons. If we are stubborn or slow to learn God's teachings, it will be a long road and perhaps one that is not completed in that lifetime.

Yes, we live many lifetimes to learn these important lessons. Some take many, many lifetimes. Others advance and learn quite quickly. It is not a competition for we are all on our own journey. It is not our job to compare ourselves and how quickly we learn, to the advances of another. We are not graded as they do in schools. We get no extra credit for advancing sooner or quicker.

Our ultimate prize is when ALL beings finish their education, as it were, and we ALL advance to the next destination or graduate to the next level as it were.

Back to the timeline.

Because God designs our timeline well before any of us ever step on Earth, it exists already. Where we go and how many lessons we learn each time is up to us.

Therefore, all the experiences have already occurred, all at once—past, present, and future. It's already been designed by God, so the order is not of any consequence. The lessons will be learned one way or another.

This is the reason that one can sometimes tap into their past or may seemingly know their future.

It all already exists.

Those who are well-tuned can tell the future or perhaps the past. Those very-well in tune can see/feel/tell past occurrences as children or even before birth. Others are able to tap into the timeline and discover previous lives. Usually this has to do with very strong yearnings or feelings that one wants to discover reasons for, or perhaps other deep, pressing questions.

All the information is available for each of us to "tap into" should we so desire.

Others may want to just live in the moment and not dwell on the past or the future. That is okay too.

There is no right way to make one's way on the journey.

But each of us must advance, however slowly it may be on this journey of life as human beings. It is our duty to God, as we promised to do our best job, and it is one's duty to the other beings, as we count on each other for our mass consciousness to be raised.

This is a wonderful way, by God's perfect design, to lift the entire planet to a new way of life—a higher consciousness—where no one is left behind.

How long it takes and what path we choose is not the point. The point is we will advance as God wishes along the joint timeline of life until the very last one has passed the finish line.

Lesson 33 - Delivery

Next, we will discuss Delivery.

Delivery of whatever we have desired and asked God for. Another word to explain this would be: God's timing.

We use "Delivery" because that is when/if God delivers your wishes to you.

You may ask for a certain thing, but it is not in your best interest. God may seemingly deny this gift, but rest assured, God will send you something far better and suitable.

Let us take this example: you are a young woman in search of love. You find a young man and you think, "Oh, he'll do," or perhaps your heart is swooning with deep desires. God knows best. He may make circumstances come about that the young man is not available and you may or may not know the reason.

All you know is he's not with you and you are heartbroken.

Do not despair, because later when you have grown and are not so needy, a more suitable man will be given to you. You may or may not realize it at the time, but you will certainly in time learn to see that God gave you a far better gift.

Not only of the man, but your own growth and maturity.

Such is the way of God. He gives us what we need, *when* we need it most—which is often not at the same moment as we express our wishes.

We must learn to accept his timing of Delivery.

Lesson 34 - Compatibility

Next let's discuss Compatibility.

This may seem like an inconsequential topic, but it is very important.

We all have a certain level of Compatibility—how we react with others and around various earthly locations, like the environment and animals.

It is important to become compatible with All That Is.

It is rude to be mean and pushy and insist on only our preferences when dealing with other people and things.

We need to show more compassion and caring in order to properly act around others.

Those characteristics lead to Compatibility, for God wants all beings and creatures here on Earth to be compatible.

Compatibility is imperative if we are to work together as one cohesive unit. We must first strive to be compatible with one another before we can truly operate as one unit.

Other lessons have been taught such as kindness and encouragement in this discourse. Many more will be explained in the continuing pages.

What we are to be aware of, is that Compatibility is imperative for our Ascension—our joint Ascension to the Heavens—as God has planned for us all.

Lesson 35 ⋅ Contemplation

Today we will learn about Contemplation.

Contemplation is when one thinks long and hard about a difficult subject matter.

We all need to learn how to do this. By Contemplation, we mean not merely a quick thought or two about something, but deep thinking on the matter.

Why does something occur? What brought it about? What are the expected consequences? Why is it important? What is it that God wants us to learn? How does this affect others?

Those sorts of thoughts—and a thinking *process*—are required for deep Contemplation.

Another method is sitting quietly and asking God or one's Spirit Guides for assistance and understanding. One's Higher Self can assist also. This requires quiet meditation and focus. Then and only then, will answers come from a Higher Power.

This process of Contemplation is required for the learning and growth God has planned for us all. Should one decide not to contemplate fully on important matters, as is their choice because of free will, then the time they spend on Earth will be lengthened; their pain and trials will be lengthened.

For we must all learn to Contemplate in order to move up the Ascension ladder and be all that we can be. All that God has envisioned for us.

Be wise my friends.

Be reflective.

Be contemplative.

It's imperative for the growth of us all, for we are all connected.

Lesson 36 ‧ Necessity

The next lesson is on Necessity.

What is necessary and why is it necessary?

Do we really *need* it, or do we merely *want* it because we don't have it at present?

These are important considerations when thinking about one's wishes.

The reason is, this is how we discover what is important and what is just a temporary desire and really frivolous. This is important for our growth as we will discover, or should be able to discover, the true value of our desires.

Does it (the desired object or action) bring us joy? Does it help mankind? Does it serve us? Does it move us forward? Or is it just whimsical?

This is not to say whimsical things are not desirable or valuable, but we need to decipher whether or not it is "just a whim."

Decoding our desires into needs and wishes helps us decide what is truly important in life. One's wishes can and will often be fulfilled. But in times of great need, we should be able to decipher which things or actions are truly a Necessity.

A Necessity is a basic need, whether it be in a human, an animal, even an object (like the care of one's home) or necessary for our home (Earth) and as such a Necessity for our environment.

We must be aware how our wishes affect our environment.

Does it cause damage—long-term or short term? Is the damage or effect valid in terms of the benefits received? Is the action one that God would have us seek?

These are all thoughts or discussions to have with yourself and possibly others when considering whether something is truly necessary.

Be kind.

Be smart.

Be contemplative when examining your desires so as to be able to identify whether they are truly necessities or merely a passing fancy or whim.

Lesson 37 · Wellness

Today we will learn about Wellness and why it's so important for our Ascension, individually and as a cohesive group.

Wellness encompasses our spiritual and physical health, for both are equally as important.

The reasons are many and here we will only explain a few, for other lessons will deal in more depth with our Physical Wellness and Spiritual Wellness.

Let's take our Physical Wellness first. Our bodies are merely units that house our very souls so that we may operate as human beings here on Earth, yet it is very important to take proper care of our bodies.

If we have an infection and we neglect to care for it, a great disease may come upon our body. Some diseases may even result in a limb or section of one's body being removed. Paying attention to one's body is imperative. Attention to our physical body is as important as attention to our outer body (the world around).

You see, both affect the Oneness of the Universe and proper care and attention to both affects the outcome and whether or not we learn the lessons necessary to ascend.

Think of this: we ignore symptoms of our body. They fester. They become worse. Then our physical health (or body) becomes ravaged by disease and we could possibly die.

God wants us to pay attention to our body and all around us. It's part of what we are here to learn. It's part of being aware. We must be aware to learn the lessons.

Spiritual Health works differently, but is equally as important, if not more important, for our Spiritual Health will affect our Physical Health.

Negative attitudes from self or others will likely result in a diminished or weary spirit of oneself, which often manifest itself in a physical affliction.

People *so* underestimate the effect of poor spiritual practices and the effect it has on one's physical body.

For instance, if your mind or spirit is filled with gluttony or excess in any way, your body will reflect this. It could show up as excess or morbid weight. It could show up as heart disease. It could show up in another way, but the first two are the most prevalent.

Let's take the example of a man who gorges himself with food, just because he can. He's wealthy and has no impending necessary tasks. He is gluttonous with his time and money—spending both to excess, only on himself.

He over-eats. He takes no action except monotonous watchings on the TV. He feels no need to help others. He doesn't tend to his spirit through meditation or prayer. He fails to direct any of his time, effort, or even thoughts toward the good or eventual lifting up of others.

Therefore, his Spiritual Wellness begins to wither so it is practically non-existent. He is undoubtedly not very happy, though he may think he's living the good life.

Eventually, this lack of a spiritual life will affect his physical body with afflictions—most likely those associated with obesity. This is from the over-indulgent of self or ego with total lack of one's spiritual growth.

Spiritual *growth* leads to Wellness of one's body and soul because these parts are interrelated. Someone who devotes hours to their spiritual practices will undoubtedly become aware enough to realize the importance of caring for their physical well-being or health.

It's all interrelated. Very important lesson to learn.

Lesson 37 · Wellness

Lesson 38 - Consciousness —
The Basics

The next lesson is on Consciousness which will be discussed in more detail throughout this discourse, but here we will touch on the basics.

Consciousness is when we are aware. Aware of our bodies, our spirits, and our souls. It is when we are aware of our surroundings, both other people and our environment (which includes animals).

We are aware through the use of our brains, a very delicate and necessary component of our bodies designed perfectly by God.

Our awareness of All That Is spurs thoughts, which evolve into our Consciousness.

A finely tuned or evolved human being will have perfected their Consciousness and ability to draw on it in times of need or inquisitiveness. One's Consciousness is a necessity if we are to evolve and be all that God desires us to be, for it all starts inside us, in our brain.

Actually, it starts in the sub-conscious mind and later advances to our conscious mind and becomes part of our Consciousness. This will be explained in further detail in future lessons.

Suffice it to say, connecting to and being aware of one's Consciousness is one of the first steps on the ladder of Ascension.

Lesson 39 ⸱ Morality

The next lesson is Morality.

Morality is the act of doing what is right because it is the right thing to do, not because man has developed laws to convince us (or encourage us) to do right. You do the right and moral thing or action not because it's what's expected or ingrained in you or even because of dire consequences.

No, you do what is right because it *is* morally right.

Society can try to structure one's actions to fit the Morality God has in mind for us, but society cannot dictate every person's every action (although it may seem like it at times).

No, God alone knows the Morality we all should follow and He, and He alone, will be the final judge.

Our Higher Self is quite aware of Morality so this is an excellent way to decipher if an action you are considering taking is actually one of higher character. Just ask your Higher Self.

If you aren't yet aware of your Higher Self, then ask God or even your spirit guides (if you are able to connect with them).

Remedies or ways to get guidance are within us all, but we must reach out to them or seek them, for actual

Morality is already known to all of us through God, as we are all One.

We may have to learn to access this information if we are just starting our spiritual path, but most of us can already "feel" or "know" if a certain action is morally correct. Only the most hedonistic don't have a clue. And they are not to be judged; they are to be pitied because they haven't yet learned.

It's the responsibility of others to set good examples for it will serve as a reminder of how one is to behave and behave properly in the world as God designed it and how to interact with others with kindness and respect.

For Morality doesn't end at the end of our body. It's a matter of how we interact with other beings in our physical world and how we interact with our environment. We all need to act with high Morality and respect for everyone and everything else because, remember, *we are all connected.*

It's part of the lesson we are to learn.

Set a great example.

Do not be swayed by the immoral and your path to God will be that much faster, for God knows the diligence one must possess in order to maintain Morality at all times.

Be moral.

Be proud.

Set an example.

Help others.

And our path to Ascension will be speedy.

Lesson 40 ‑ **Rumors**

This lesson is on Rumors.

Listen not to others who speak poorly of your friends. Instead listen to your friends and help them in times of need, for you never know the true trials another person is encountering.

Rumors spread like wildfire and can be equally as dangerous. We think nothing of it when we drop a little hint or innuendo, much like one might inadvertently drop a lit match.

But the damage can be quite the same—ruined lives, damaged homes, feelings of loss and betrayal. Yet all this disaster is easily avoided.

All one has to do is stop the Rumors—or don't start them—just like you do not pass a lit torch and do not light a torch, for we don't know the whole story about others. We might *think* we know, or we speculate. We spread these unsubstantiated "truths" to others, and they spread to others until it seems to many in society that the Rumor is true, when in fact, it is not.

Do *not* fall victim to this demeaning and demoralizing practice. This is definitely *not* what God would want.

First of all, it is judging, which is reserved for God alone.

Second of all, we as humans do not know all the facts—we just surmise.

So to spread these untruths is very disingenuous. It serves no purpose other than the entertainment of those gossiping. This is not how God wants us to act.

Instead, He prefers we reach out to those people who appear to be doing something wrong and ask if we can help. Do they need our guidance or perhaps our money or maybe they only need a friend—not someone spreading Rumors about them that may make their journey even harder than it needs to be?

Remember our journey is to grow and learn ourselves. Helping others to grow and learn is to be expected, but to hinder others through Rumors and other spiteful ways does not meet the level of morality God has set for us.

Lesson 41 - Fatigue

Fatigue is a sign of lack of well-being—both in the physical body and in the mind.

We need to recognize when we are fatigued and take proper steps to defeat it.

Most often Physical Fatigue is experienced when one lacks enough sleep.

Reason sleep is so imperative. Without sufficient sleep, one is unable to complete the required tasks, both properly or correctly and in the required time period.

It's important to listen to our bodies and make time to get enough sleep.

The other type of Fatigue is Spiritual Fatigue—when one's spirit or mind is not afforded enough rest.

Quiet time or meditation helps with this. Proper fuel or nutrition is a help also, for our mind and our brain need sufficient sustenance just like our bodies, or they start to show or exhibit Fatigue. Continued Spiritual Fatigue can be disastrous for it leads to poor choices which often leads to delayed advancement.

Best to learn to identify one's Fatigue and address it properly, sooner than later.

*Lesson 42 - More on Compatibility

Today's lesson is on Compatibility.

One must learn to be compatible with all earthly creatures – both humans and animals. The reason you know by now through this discourse is that *we are all connected.* Connected as one vibrant, living entity.

When one part is injured or hurt, it affects another.

Ever wonder how your loving pets, especially a dog, can sense when you are upset? They tend to comfort you. That is how they show their love to you in times of need.

Ever wonder how the sky sends a rainbow seemingly just to you, at the perfect time? That is the environment heeding your needs.

We must learn to accept and rejoice in the fact *we are all one* with everything. It is a miraculous thing that God has created for us. A wonderous miracle to be sure.

Embrace this occurrence or way of life, as it is all part of God's plan.

We must learn how to be compatible (get along) with others. It will bring us joy—as well as God—for it means we are learning our lessons here on Earth.

Compatibility with the environment is also required. We must take care that our actions (or lack of actions) do not interfere with the environment. This too will please God.

It is the being "aware" that will lend itself to "Compatibility." A very important lesson to learn.

Lesson 43 - Novelty

On to Novelty.

It may seem like an odd topic, but I will explain. You see, before Earth was created, all matter or energy was in a different form.

God developed His great plan and transformed the energy into the Earth and all the beings and creatures and outdoor wonder.

It became a *Novelty*—a new experience. It brought God happiness and joy. All the "newness" was quite wonderful, even to Him.

So God understands Novelty or newness or uniqueness, as it were.

This is something we should all learn to accept and embrace also.

Some humans see newness in things or events and become withdrawn or scared, but they lack the ability to see the Novelty in the situation.

If we learn to see the Novelty and embrace it, we are more likely to strive for newness and thus experience a bolder and more expansive life here on Earth. This helps one grow and learn, which in turn, swiftens our advancement.

So you can see one's ability to embrace Novelty is a good thing, one that helps us advance to all that God wants for us.

Let us not forget to smile and be happy when we experience Novelty, be it in small or large ways.

Lesson 44 - Testament

Testament.

This is *very* important. This is when we give statements as to our beliefs.

People may be shy to do so, but this serves as verification to others that their feelings are right.

They might be apprehensive or even afraid to share their beliefs, but the viewing or listening to another's testament will spur them along.

Ever notice how one's actions or words can affect another? This works in the same way. We are constantly searching and looking to others for answers. When we hear their Testament, those deep, heartfelt words become embedded in our souls and part of us. Such words spur us along.

We give Testament or make bold statements, which is what Testament is, others listen and look up to us. Then the process expands.

This is how God planned our existence. This is one of the many ways God planned for us to learn and grow together, using each other's wisdom to advance.

Do not be remiss and forget to listen to the Testament of others and to develop and share your Testament. For it is this joint effort that will move this planet forward.

A very important action and lesson indeed.

Lesson 45 · Compatibility and Vibrations

Compatibility is our lesson today.

Ever wonder why some people are more compatible with society and others are not? It is because they are well-acquainted with God's way.

Let us explain. When we first came here none of us were compatible with each other or nature or other animals. In time, we learned to be Compatible or "get along with each other," as it were.

How is this accomplished you ask? Well, it is by following God's ways or God's commandments. If one doesn't follow God's ways, one will not be Compatible with those around him, living or deceased.

It has to do with vibrational frequency.

You may have learned by now, that in order to be on a good vibrational frequency, one that is calm and centered where life "flows," one must be living solely or nearly completely by following God's commandments.

This requires not only behaving or acting according to God's wishes, but also by surrendering to God and letting *him* lead the way. This doesn't mean you are not exercising "free will." Quite the opposite actually.

It means one exercises his free will and *chooses* to follow God's ways.

Once these mental and physical actions are taken, one becomes more relaxed and calmer, which aids to being on the right, or a better, vibrational mode.

Once one is on a good vibrational frequency, life and interactions with others are greatly improved. You might say you are more "in tune" with each other.

Being "in tune" means you are more compatible. Compatibility is therefore something to be strived for. It is very important for living a better life, a more God-centered life and a life that will bring peace and joy not only to oneself, but to the world around him.

Remember:

Relaxing, Calming, Surrender →

Correct Vibrational Frequency →

A Life of Flow and Ease →

Compatibility with Others →

Following God's Way →

Path to Ascension

Once learned and absorbed into one's life, the reminder would be like this:

Calm → *Good Vibrations* → *Good Compatibility* →

God's Way → *Path to Ascension*

Compatibility means nothing more than getting along with others, but it must be done in a way of peace and harmony for it to lead to eventual Ascension.

Lesson 45 - Compatibility and Vibrations

Lesson 46 - Ascension

L et us explain more about Ascension, which is the path to becoming more God-like.

True, Ascension means to lift higher, but there is a bit more to it in the spiritual realm.

We are all called here to Earth with a covenant to God: our promise to do our very best.

Each lifetime may not hold a monumental mission; however, we *are* required to learn and grow. In order to do so, we must give our best effort.

Learning will eventually put us on the path to Ascension, which is becoming a better person morally (through our actions and thoughts). As we learn God's lessons, we absorb them. They become part of our being, morally.

We learn to interact well with others (be more compatible).

We are in tune with the environment and consider our actions among it.

We feel compassion for others, and it affects our actions.

There are many, many lessons which will be explained or have been explained or touched on so far in this discourse.

The main thing we are to learn is that we are One with everything.

We are One with All That Is.

Such learning will put us on the path of Ascension, where we become more conscious of our interactions, raise our vibrational mode (even collectively) and eventually rise to the Heavens above to join one's Archangels and other spiritual leaders.

Our God-like actions and beliefs will lead to Ascension, which is God's eventual goal for us all.

How long it takes—and what route we take—is determined by our free will, but we will all eventually make the path to Ascension as God has planned.

It is written in stone and will be repeated in many new and wonderous places within our great Universe and beyond; far too difficult for us to understand at this moment in time.

But it will occur, and re-occur, time and again nonetheless.

It brings joy to God each time one of us ascends. It brings Him joy when we make even small steps—no matter how small it is—towards our eventual goal of Ascension.

It will be a joyous time for all once mankind has ascended to the Heavens together and joined with God, even though it is a somewhat temporary occasion, because eventually the cycle will repeat itself as we continue to learn to be a more evolved society or group of collective beings acting as "One."

Be blessed, be wise, for we, your Archangels are always here to guide you on this journey. All one must do is "Ask." More on that in another discourse.

Suffice it to say, we are all here on a journey of Ascension and should strive to help each other achieve it.

For we will not go to the last iteration until the last being has learned the lessons, and all have ascended above as God wishes/desires and has planned eons ago.

Lesson 46 - Ascension

Lesson 47 · Hightower

Next lesson is Hightower, which is the action of putting God first in your beliefs and actions.

This is a simple step, but it must not come solely from one's actions. It must come from one's heart.

One must put God first, not just because it is the right thing to do, but because it *feels* right, and one *wants* to do so.

By putting God first, we are talking about doing in actions as God would want us to do— following his covenants for a good and faithful life or existence here on Earth.

Those who don't put God first or make progress toward putting God first, will have many incarnations here on Earth before they are allowed to ascend. Reason we all need to pay attention to those lessons presented to us.

The name Hightower may seem odd to new followers, but the name has been around for a long time. It is a symbol of a biblical place—a tower or monument—high on a mountain where one looks up to God.

A place to pray. A place to connect. A sacred place. A place to be revered, just like God.

Our daily lives are greatly improved when we act in accordance with the Hightower, giving glory to God and following His requirements for a good and worthy life—

one where we all do our best, and encourage others to do their best, and therefore mankind's best effort will be put forth.

Lesson 48 - Refreshing One's Soul

Refreshing one's soul is an important activity to learn. Certainly one necessary for Ascension. You see, one cannot advance if one is not routinely refreshed and cleansed in one's soul.

It helps in one's soul development—which is what happens when we learn and grow.

If one's soul is clean and clear, the lessons are more easily captured or learned.

When one's soul is full of worry and doubt and other congestive feelings, it is unable to have room for growth. It is stuck or congested like a pipe. It must be clear for God's healing powers to enter and do their work. Using this physical "picture" may help to understand visually. Nonetheless, this is how it works.

Now, how does one refresh their soul, or cleanse their soul, so they are ready to accept the word of God in written form or by lessons?

First, one must *want* to listen to God and learn.

Second, one must relax and be in a state of calmness so they are prepared to *receive* the word.

Third, one must *listen* intently or pay attention.

It is not a difficult process, but it must be adhered to. Failure to follow these steps will not likely lead to success. Diligence in following these criteria will almost certainly make one successful.

Now, how does one slow down enough to listen to God? There are many, many ways on this part.

Some people enjoy a walk in nature for it has a calming effect and one's worries are forgotten when walking among God's majestic nature—or at least one's worries are greatly diminished or put in perspective.

Others find that prayer or meditation will refresh their souls and put them in the proper mindset to hear God's word. Some follow a specific ritual such as candles or scents designed to cleanse one's mind or soul, as it were.

Some beings find a sports activity helps them. Through strict concentration, they are able to clear away all the debris inside their soul and make room for new, better thoughts. Examples are yoga, Pilates, cycling, running/jogging, hiking, and rowing. These activities can combine nature with them, making it even more valuable for refreshing one's soul.

This is the reason when people find an activity they like, they tend to stick with it. It's not just the physical well-being or improvements, but the soul-cleansing or refreshing that is occurring.

Even sex can be such an activity. However, there are special circumstances for this method to be an activity that refreshes one's soul. The reason is, this is a sacred activity between a man and a woman and should not be taken in a recreational manner. It will be discussed in a later lesson as it is a very important lesson indeed.

In summary, one must discover—or uncover—the methods that seem successful to them that will refresh and cleanse their soul so they are ready to learn the ways of God. It opens them up to accepting or learning that is not possible without a refreshed soul.

God's desire is that we make it a habit to cleanse our soul daily, so it becomes habit, and such a deeply ingrained habit that it becomes a constant existence, one that never leaves us. In such a state, one is living and breathing the word of God through one's body.

One is an open vessel, constantly ready to receive the word/the lesson.

One's soul is virtually always refreshed, clear, and clean.

In such a state, one serves as an example to others of what can be achieved: the happiness, the flow, and the light will be easily recognizable for all to see.

This state is only possible if one refreshes their soul.

A very important lesson for one to learn and has an effect not just on one's individual Ascension, but on the Ascension to all mankind because remember, *we are all connected.*

Lesson 49 - Connectedness to Each Other

Connectedness to Each Other is the next lesson.

Let us first explain how and why we are all connected as beings, living a human existence, for those who may not be familiar with this concept.

There is a notion that "I am a separate person or being from all others and I can do whatever I wish. I don't need God or anyone else."

Yet, in this scenario, let's imagine what happens when one falls ill. It's likely one would seek out a doctor or at least a friend to console them. This shows Connectedness, for without such interaction one could be all alone and not connected to others.

Think about one's family—a spouse or children. Their effect on one's life surely shows Connectedness.

Even those without a spouse or children have the family they were born into, which may or may not be a strong bond.

Even those estranged from families they were born into eventually develop a friend or two who become like family and they are connected to them.

The human condition requires at least some minimal contact with others for survival and our psychological needs. These needs exist even among those who consider themselves "hermits," for they are still surviving on the fruits of another human's labor, such as roads, electricity, buildings, food, transportation, and medical assistance.

No man can truly exist without the Connectedness to others.

How and why this happens is quite a miraculous feat.

God designed us to be interconnected so we could learn lessons and grow. He wants all beings to ascend together as one unit eventually.

Scientifically or metaphysically, there are also reasons. We are connected by unseen lines that shape our lives and interactions.

Some beings have strong ties to others. This is our soul group, our tribe, or our soul community. These are folks we feel a strong connection with, even if we don't understand why. More about this concept later. Suffice it to say we are closer to some people than others.

Other people are brought into our lives to teach us lessons or vice versa or perhaps even both are to learn lessons. These people could be a family member or someone you meet on life's journey. We connect and interact for some period of time during our lifetime.

Our actions and inactions truly have an effect or consequence on others that we can observe daily. When you watch the news there is no lack of horrendous activities that affect others, such as murders, accidents, illnesses, or disease.

Even those occurrences that seem to affect only one person do not.

For example, if someone commits suicide it may seem to only affect them, but the family is affected by the loss. If there's no family there is undoubtedly, medical and police personnel who are affected by such a trauma. So you see, no man exists alone in a vacuum.

We all are connected to others and more deeply so than most are aware of.

Lesson 50 - Connectedness to the Environment

In the previous lesson we explained man's connectedness to each other. Connectedness to the Environment must also be understood. This is the topic for this lesson.

First of all, one must understand that the Environment is a living and breathing creation. It was created by God to interact with us, to be connected to us in ways we might not have been aware of in the beginning of our existence.

We may think the environment is here for the taking and we can abuse it and take all we want. This is not the case, for our very interaction with the environment has an effect on our lives.

For instance, if we take all the water and divert it for useless reasons, then we will feel the effect one day of lack of water. And it will be our own doing!

If we harness the sunshine to create energy, this is a good and wise interaction. Sunshine is never depleted, there is just more or less on given days. Using this environmental resource in a wise way can be beneficial to us as humans. It shows we are connected.

Everything we do outside has an effect on the environment from pulling a small weed in our garden (which will then never grow) to carving out the side of a mountain, for when that occurs, water doesn't flow off the mountain in the same manner affecting streams below, affecting fish and other species. The effects continue and continue.

Can you see now how we are Connected to the Environment?

We hope you will open up and realize how your very existence affects those around you, both people and the Environment.

We are not alone.

All actions (or inactions) do not only relate to us.

We are deeply interwoven into the lives of others. We must act accordingly, for there is more to this great Universe than merely our solo existence (or what we depict as a solo existence) for we are not alone.

We are actually already one cohesive unit, learning to operate as One. In order to do so, we must follow the word of God and other Great Masters and develop a kindness and respect for the environment because it is really just a part—albeit a large part—of us and our existence here on Earth.

Lesson 51 ‑ Character

Today's lesson is on Character and the ability to do as one says and why it's important.

In the beginning of man's existence here on Earth, Character was somewhat lacking because man was focused mainly on survival. When push came to shove, man's choices were made according to what he needed or wanted, not according to what was fair or just.

In time, man realized a need to be nicer to others. (You can see now how man's growth takes so long.)

At any rate, he realized he couldn't always take from others and that in order to live in peace and harmony with his tribe, he had to act in a more caring manner.

Rules of connection, or morals, were developed, and man began to be more conscious of how his behaviors affected others in his tribe. He could get along better with his tribe members if they all adhered to these rules or moral codes.

These rules, however, did not extend to other tribes. It was like a barrier or wall. Those within his walls were treated one way, but those on the outside were looked upon with disdain and fear.

Eventually some men developed the Character and wisdom necessary to afford others outside the clan with the same moral code. Some are still working on this as we speak. Some are less developed and therefore slower to learn these lessons.

One's Character comes to mind in these situations. Character is what one is made of – the qualities of one's beliefs and the constitution to follow through on those beliefs.

Let's take this example: a man goes to the local market or trading post with wares to sell or barter with. He wants to buy or trade his item for that of another. He wants a fair price for his item but isn't willing to pay a fair price for another's.

His moral Character is somewhat blemished. He's willing to pay another for their goods —just not very much, yet he wants the full benefit of his items. Most would look from the outside and say this isn't fair. Yet the man, knowing how desperate the other one is, will offer a lower price; so low in fact, to the level that the other man is insulted yet must take the amount even though the value is very low, just because his family is in dire need.

Some would say the second man has been taken advantage of; some would say that's just how it works.

Some barter is acceptable, especially in certain cultures and even somewhat expected; but as a general rule, to try to barter so low to hinder or hurt the one offering a product can be considered cheating.

One of good moral Character would never stoop so low as to expect top dollar for his item and yet pay others only a paltry amount. This man knows all men have families to feed and isn't concerned or desirous of making the second man suffer. He innately wants to be fair.

This is how God wants man to behave: fairly—in his interactions with others, whether they are in his tribe or another community. He wants man to be fair and act with consciousness and caring when interacting with others. Such actions are a measure of one's Character.

Character must be developed. It is usually learned in one's family or at least in one's tribe. How you treat others is often the result of how they treat you. It's learned from the group.

For this reason, it is so important that parents and others set good high moral standards so the offspring can observe such Character in others and act accordingly.

This is, and has been, a struggle for mankind through the ages: how to develop a sustainable society without infringing on the rights of others outside their tribe.

Take for example the Indians in North America. When the white man first came, he wanted to take over their lands. There was no thought of peaceful coexistence. It was just take, take, take.

Eventually the white man learned he must make amends and offered some solace to the Indians, through payments and land. But even these efforts were too little, too late, for the treacherous deed he had performed. But it was a way to learn lessons—on both sides—and hopefully both parties will learn and grow from the experience.

The white man will someday learn (if he hasn't already), that he is not superior to others and it is not within his rights to take that of another.

Perhaps the Indians will learn methods so as not to be taken advantage of again. Both will learn. Both will grow. Their Characters will be melded into men with greater understanding and ability to follow better moral codes.

This is what God intends for us: improved moral codes and stronger Character, even in difficult times, for the true test of one's Character is in more difficult times.

The true test of one's moral Character is if one does the right thing because it's *right*, not because someone is watching.

One must have high moral Character if one desires to ascend. It is such a commandment (or requirement) and one we should all endeavor to learn to the best of our abilities.

Lesson 52 · Atonement

This lesson is on Atonement: the repenting and making amends for one's transgressions or lack of character.

No man is perfect. We all should be trying to be better, the best we can be, or as one might say, trying to be perfect. But we fail. We make mistakes.

Some of these are grievous errors for which we must repent for our wrongdoing.

This is what Atonement is all about. When one's actions are morally reprehensible, one needs to recognize the error of his ways and make amends.

These amends must be directed to those who experienced the wrongdoing. These amends must be heartfelt and sincere. The amends must be worthy. In other words, they must fit the "crime" as it were (be of equal value). For if an amend is only half-hearted, it will not be accepted by God.

Our heart must be willing, and not just an act to say we did it.

Atonement must be made from a sense of kindness and caring and heart-felt repentance for one's past errors.

One's actions must speak louder than words. Merely saying you'll make amends is not the point. It's the *doing* to make amends that's important. It's all part of one's character if one is to follow through. No follow-through, then one's character is yet to be developed fully.

It's one thing to recognize the need to atone, it's quite another to take the action to follow through.

God requires *both* for your growth and eventual Ascension.

Lesson 53 · Sincerity

Sincerity is a humbling and important lesson to learn. One must feel sincere when making amends, dealing with others and even loving others.

Sincerity comes from the heart.

Many may appear to be sincere, but their heart is not in it and therefore they are only pretending to be sincere. God wants all men to learn to be sincere in their actions. If they aren't sincere, then perhaps they shouldn't even do the action, for others will eventually see through them and that can present a whole other set of circumstances.

If one is not sincere in their actions, their very character is called into question. Others start to doubt their very word. Their actions cannot be trusted. How they deal with others is called into question, even in those situations where they *were* sincere.

See how all this works?

Our thoughts affect our actions, which build (or destroys) our character. Character-building is an important process and Sincerity is at the base or root of it.

Remember this lesson as you go through your journey in life. It will serve you well.

Sincerity leads to proper actions, which build strong character.

Sincerity →

Proper Actions →

Strong Character

Lesson 54 · Relationships

Today we are going to speak about Relationships, those between humans and between humans and their God.

When God created Earth and put humans on it, He envisioned sweet and loving Relationships between the beings. He knew this would not be automatic upon their creation. He knew it would be a process, an evolution of sorts, where man would learn and grow and eventually become more loving and kinder to each other.

He knew there would be strife. There would be pain. There would be highs and lows, and ups and downs on this journey of building good Relationships between men.

Much progress has been made since the beginning when Relationships were much more volatile than they are now. However, mankind still has far to go to become the loving and kind unit that God desires.

His lessons are the way we are shaped to become more kind and loving and intertwined with each other.

One's Relationship with God is quite another matter. We all have our own path in that regard too. Some are educated about God in their upbringing, which can be most helpful for it is all they have ever known. They grow in acceptance and belief of their Relationship with God.

Others are indoctrinated into their church at an early age, but do not accept or follow the teachings. That method of early exposure to God doesn't work for them.

They and other non-believers must come to discover God in a multitude of other ways as they go on their path of life. God hopes they will come to know Him on each of their visits to Earth; however, this may or may not happen due to free will.

Man's Relationship with God is paramount to Ascension, as is a man's Relationship with others. It's that Connectedness that spurs along the process of Ascension, for no man, woman, or being will ascend without a caring Relationship for others and a close understanding with God.

Man's Relationship with others and how they are all connected is a lesson man must be willing to learn in order to ascend.

Man's Relationship with God must be developed—and adhered to also—if one is to ascend and complete God's vision of all kindred souls ascending to the Heavens.

God knows it is well within the capabilities of all of us to have these Relationships and He guides us through the many lessons presented to us during our lives here on Earth. It is up to us to learn the lessons.

Lesson 55 - Ramifications

The next topic is Ramifications or Results/Consequences.

We all know by now that there are consequences to our various actions. Part of what we learn here on Earth is the consequences of our actions or even inactions.

How we interact with *others* has certain Ramifications. How we interact with the *world* around us has certain Ramifications.

Let us take this example. A man is walking down the street. He sees a young boy with a ball, kicking it down the street. He yells at the boy, "Get out of the street. You don't belong there."

The Ramifications are that the boy is now robbed of his joy of playing with the ball and his thoughts are on the grumpy or unfriendly man. The man is centered on thoughts like, "Oh, that stupid boy. How could he play in the street?"

Both of their days have been tainted. This has been the Ramification of the man's thoughtless remarks.

Now, let's take another eye to the same circumstances. The man sees the boy playing in the street and he joins in the game. The boy laughs at the man trying to play, as it was quite unexpected.

The man returns to his inner child and is young in feelings and thoughts once again. Both leave the encounter with quite a *different* feeling: one of upliftment, joy, and happiness.

This is the result God would wish for us to learn: how to interact with others and have a kind and loving result versus Ramifications that hurt each other's soul or damage one's spirit.

It's up to each of us to determine which Ramification of each situation we will impart on others. It's up to us to learn the lessons. It's up to us to leave others with a feeling of joy and happiness, or at the very minimum, leave them better off than when we first encountered them.

Lesson 56 · Happiness

This lesson is on Happiness.

It is true: Happiness—true Happiness—is already within each of us. It is our job to uncover or discover how to bring it to the surface.

We all have the same ups and downs in life, although it may not appear so if we are comparing our lives to others. But we all have trials that we think rob us of our joy and Happiness.

Yes, certain events and thus lessons, may change our gauge or expectation of Happiness, but one of the things we are to learn is how to be happy throughout the bad times. We learn how to do this by seeking Happiness within.

Such Happiness can be achieved in a variety of ways. One can focus on the "good" in a situation versus the "bad." That's the equivalent of looking on the bright or positive side. One remains happy even in a less-than-desirable situation by looking at the situation in a positive light.

Another way, usually helpful in more difficult times, is to realize that God is teaching you a lesson and become thankful for that lesson.

This could be in a situation of severe loss of say a dear loved one, such as through death or long separation. You might have a terrible loss and be quite unhappy, but by appreciating the time you *did* have with your loved one, it can bring you some sense of Happiness. The Happiness may be through your tears, but you *can* be happy, even in such a situation.

It's up to us how we choose to observe each situation in life as to whether or not we will be happy. It's all up to us.

Learning God's lessons will facilitate these lessons. We can learn, or condition our minds, to become happier.

Happiness—true Happiness within—is required for Ascension. For one cannot ascend if one is not a happy being, filled with love and concern for others as well as himself.

It's a covenant with God that we promised to learn here on Earth.

Lesson 57 · Timeliness

Today's lesson is on Timeliness.

You may wonder why and if it is important to be timely. The answer is yes, because even though time is not on a straight line as humans generally think, Timeliness can and does change everything.

Take this common example. If you don't go to a specific location at a specific time, you might not encounter a person or situation that may or may not change your life.

Think of the person who happens by a store or coffee shop, meets an old friend, and rekindles their romance and later spends many years together.

Think of a teacher or grandparent who teaches an important lesson to a child that is then known, absorbed, and followed their entire life.

These supposedly chance meetings are the result of Timeliness.

When God is ready to teach you such lessons, then circumstances will be put in place. What is your role in these happenings?

To be aware.

To listen.

To follow His commandments and be open to the results.

If you hear a voice in your head telling you to stop by a little music store and look for a sheet of music, do so. There is likely someone for you to encounter there. Perhaps someone whose day you can brighten—or a future friend. These are your Archangels guiding you on behalf of God.

Think about another instance. Your child is ill, extremely ill. You are busy at work or home and do not tend to their needs. The child's condition worsens and by the time you take the child to the hospital, it is too late to save them or perhaps the illness or injury is exacerbated.

We must all pay attention and be timely in our actions.

To be timely leads one more quickly on the path of Ascension. Those who do not pay attention and act in a timely manner will take longer to learn and advance. It's okay if that happens, but we as your Archangels want you to know it is within your power to move things along if you so desire.

God will ensure the lessons be learned prior to Ascension; you just may have a different path to get there.

Lesson 58 · Fidelity

Today's lesson is on Fidelity, being true to one's promise.

Usually humans think of Fidelity as being true to one's spouse, but it has other meanings which we'll discuss here.

Fidelity is the practice of doing what you say and being true to one's ideals or core beliefs.

If you believe in water conservation, then you need to act accordingly and not waste water. This is practicing Fidelity.

If you go to church and espouse to follow their core beliefs, then you must practice those beliefs even when you are not in the big house.

It's important to do as you say. This builds character and trust with others. It is not always easy to do so. At times, we are all tempted to take the easy way, but we mustn't do so.

God requires we learn how to practice Fidelity as part of Ascension. Do try your best until it becomes a habit and a natural way of being to you. This is the action God desires of us all.

Lesson 59 - Remembrance

This lesson is on Remembrance.

We all need to remember important people in our lives for their very lessons learned will aid and assist us in our growth, but only if we make a point to remember them.

Remember those words of wisdom from a grandparent or a teacher? Or a lesson your parent taught you? This is what we are referring to.

We also need to remember the actions or the stories of what occurred.

Let's say Johnnie rode off on his motorcycle without a helmet in the pouring rain, after a tiff with his girlfriend. Tragedy struck. When we remember this incident we feel sorry for Johnnie, his family, and his girl. We should also remember not to go off in a huff when upset and to take proper precautions, like a helmet and follow road signs, lest tragedy strike us too.

This is what Remembrance means.

Another example, and humans do this one well, is to remember those who lost their lives in times of battle. This is an important process—almost a continuous grieving process—that goes on for future generations. This is a wonderful way to teach lessons to younger folks who did not experience the wars.

Through Remembrance, we all remember, young and old, the sacrifices made.

One hope is by such action, humans will note the cost of battle and refrain from it. Another result is the deep caring for other people. God wishes us to experience both through Remembrance of others.

The same can be said for various religious practices which the purpose of it is to remember. Such as the birth of Christ and the Resurrection.

Other religions have equally important celebrations and it is their way of Remembrance. It is not our job to criticize their religion, but merely accept that they too, have a way to remember important events and thus are also practicing Remembrance. Such actions help all mankind to learn and grow together, as one unit.

This is how God designed us and is our natural way. Through Remembrance, we are able to celebrate our Connectedness.

Lesson 60 - Sexuality

Let's begin our discussion of Sexuality, an important and most curious discussion to most humans.

It may not be the discourse one expects.

First of all, God made man and woman in his image, which is a spirit image, not even one that we can see with our eyes. It's an image or entity that is only felt, but it exists nonetheless. More on that concept at a later time.

The body of a man was designed to complement the body of the woman. The man is full of masculine energy which complements the woman's feminine energy. Their sexual body parts complement each other and have compartments and extensions making it possible for them to connect in a very personal and sacred way.

Being in possession of these sacred body parts is their Sexuality, for such a connection in the physical sense would not be possible without these anatomical situations.

God formed man and woman in such a physical manner for these reasons:

1. For procreation, as this is how humans are able to reproduce.
2. To form strong, sacred, and lasting connections between a man and a woman. These connections are acknowledged by the church as eternal vows.

3. To instill a feeling of connectedness and love between a man and woman, such a connectedness they do not share with others.
4. To give humans the opportunity to love another deeply, more than themselves.

These are the core reasons for our Sexuality. There are more to be sure, but these are the main reasons.

We all should accept and celebrate our own Sexuality for this is how God created us. We need to learn how to act, learn, and grow according to the bodies we've been given.

Some may be perplexed and experience various challenges with their Sexuality.

This is their journey and their lessons to learn. It may be a seemingly somewhat different path than what others experience, but it is just more "noticeable" to others.

We all have our own journey, even in the sexual arena. The degree of difference is of no concern for we are each on our own path of self-discovery and yearning for completion through Sexuality.

God has a plan for each of us. Our Sexuality is part of the plan. No two people have exactly the same plan or path to follow, even if similarities exist.

Remember, the goal of Sexuality is to bring each of us closer to God in the end.

We will experience a fuller, more loving life through our Sexuality than we would have otherwise. It's one of the many miracles of our very creation, a miracle designed by God to help us learn and grow to be all that we can be.

Treasure your Sexuality for it's a gift from God. It's part of what makes you, YOU. We are all a bit different, yet we are all the same…one Connected unit and Sexuality brings us there.

Lesson 60 - Sexuality

Lesson 61 ‧ Resilience

The word today is Resilience.

We must all learn to be resilient during our journey on Earth. The reasons are many.

We will face many challenges.

We must learn to cope; to rise above them and seek higher ground, seek a better path. This is what Resilience is all about.

God wants us to rise above the challenges, conquer them, and move on to new heights. Then, and only then, will we be able to understand the words of God.

It's through our enduring ability to meet challenges or situations presented to us that we grow to be the type of beings that God desires.

How do we do this?

First, we must have faith in God and His way and His decisions. We must believe that all we do and all that we go through is for a greater cause: to learn and grow to be all we can be.

Then we must trust in God that all will work out. Faith gets us started; trust keeps us going.

We must have the ending belief that the best possible outcome for us is on its way to us. This is how one develops Resilience, with the help of our Almighty God.

Now, this is not to diminish the assistance of other beings, for they are, and can be, a great help too. But one must put their faith, trust, and belief in God to start or continue the process. That's how it all works.

When you are down and facing a challenge, look within, look to God, and look to others as a way to rise above. Your Heavenly Father is always with you so be sure to ask him for guidance when you need it.

We hope these clues have been most helpful to you and you will draw upon our guidance as you travel your path here on Earth.

Lesson 62 · Turning Points

This lesson is on Turning Points, which are defining moments in our lives in which we change our course.

God sends us these situations to make us realize a change is due.

If we heed His suggestion, we will turn our lives around so to speak, and seek a new direction in life.

It's very important to listen when these circumstances come into existence. To ignore them usually means a more *severe* Turning Point in the future. And if still ignored, then an equally severe situation will rear its head in the future.

Better to pay attention and redirect your route at the earliest opportunity. Listening to one's self and taking time for reflection will help you be more "in tune" and better able to sense when such changes or redirections are necessary.

Listening for answers during prayer time from your Archangels would be helpful too, to help identify when a change of course is needed. Of course, one can always pray directly to God for guidance also.

The important part is to be aware.

Draw on your senses.

Ask for guidance.

These systems will aid in your discovering when its necessary to make a change in your direction in life.

You will learn even more when you embark on the next journey or path, as you change course. Your old problems may seem weak compared to the ones you encounter on the new path, but you will grow. You will grow indeed, into the being or type of being God wishes for us all.

Be open to these changes in your direction offered by your individual life's Turning Points, for they are to be embraced and appreciated as opportunities to improve one's life.

Don't be afraid or timid to seek the new, untrodden path, for it will lead you somewhere wonderful even if you must go through fire to get there.

Our covenant with God before our arrival on Earth is to do our best to learn and grow. Accepting the challenges when these Turning Points are presented to us is one way we can show God we will follow through on our promises.

Lesson 63 - Routines

Next, we'll discuss the following of Routines.

This may seem like a nonsensical topic, but we will herewith explain its importance and a very important concept it is indeed.

Routines help us establish the basis of our lives. The ease of following a routine helps us focus on new things.

Let us explain. If you have a basic everyday routine, you don't have to think about when to get up, what to eat, where to go, what to do, because you have a regular Routine.

Imagine how much effort it would take just to make those decisions anew each day. It would be insurmountable to get that far daily. There would be no time or ability (strength) left in you to make the harder, more difficult choices necessary for real development of your soul. You'd remain "stuck" in your daily existence.

Unfortunately, some humans do remain stuck, never reaching the potential that God has before them. These people will undoubtedly repeat their journeys until such time as they "wake up" and start paying attention and learn the lessons put forth.

One way to do this—actually an imperative way—is to have Routines. Routines for your own morning, the way you keep your home, the way you act at work, the way you interact with others and your family traditions.

Life is complicated enough. Establish good Routines; follow them and there will be plenty of time and ability to "learn the lessons."

This is an important concept to grasp and one that will greatly aid in one's development here on Earth.

Lesson 64 ⸱ Trust

Today we will explain about the importance of Trust — Trust among each other and trusting in God.

One's Trust points to the core of one's character.

If others don't Trust you, you are somewhat a tainted person, for their interactions with you are somewhat diminished or incomplete.

Because if you are not held in a place of complete Trust, you are unable to fulfill your life's mission. Others are reluctant to participate with you. You cannot obtain the full glory of knowing and connecting with others. Your connection is incomplete or broken.

You see, Trust is the glue that holds our relationships together.

No Trust, no deep relationship. Deep Trust, then deep relationship.

How can we all be as "One" if we don't trust each other?

Think of this example. A man tells his wife he'll be home at 6:00 pm to attend a family function, such as a birthday event for their child. He doesn't show up. He arrives home at 9:00 pm, all disheveled and says he worked late. Yet, he smells of woman's perfume and has been drinking.

The wife knows he has lied and doesn't Trust him. The children are oblivious to the clues but feel a lack of Trust none the less.

All they know is they counted on father to be there for an important event and he didn't. They feel rejected and unimportant. They start to lose Trust in their father's ability to keep his word.

They wonder if they can count on him.

They wonder if he loves them.

You can see how repeated episodes would lead to a complete lack of Trust. The relationship crumbles because there is no glue—no Trust—binding it together.

One's family is the first place we learn Trust. Later, as we grow, we learn to Trust teachers and friends and others we encounter on life's path.

Some of us are naturally trusting and when other people let us down, it can be incredibly difficult to handle. Others are naturally timid and untrusting, perhaps due to our upbringing or just our natural proclivities. We may have a hard time trusting others at all.

Nonetheless, all of us must learn to Trust and be Trustworthy on this journey. It is part of what we are here to learn.

The other part we are to learn is to Trust God. Trust His way and Trust His timing.

This concept in itself presents quite a challenge for many, especially those who know what they want and want it NOW. God's timing is always perfect, so we need to learn to give in to his timing or accept that his timing will be perfect.

Ask the child waiting for a special surprise or gift. He's anxious and cannot wait. Begs daily for his "prize." But God knows the exact moment that is best and even if the highly awaited item is even the right item for the child. Perhaps something else would be much more appropriate.

God know these things and will bring the perfect object, person, or situation to us exactly at the right time. We just need to learn to Trust Him.

It's all part of our growth process here on Earth.

It's why we are all here: to learn and grow and become even more connected.

Trust is one of the paths to achieving the Miracle of Connectedness.

Lesson 64 · Trust

Lesson 65 - Righteousness

Today's lesson is on Righteousness.

God's power is Righteous.

It is not a power to be contended with. It is all-knowing and all-powerful. The deeds are always right, even if it doesn't seem so.

Let us give you some examples. The man whose home burns down is then required to work incredibly hard to attain the difficult task of caring for his family and rebuilding his home. This is the experience God wants him to go through so he'll learn and grow and be all he can be. You can imagine how much stronger the man will be after accomplishing this feat, can you not?

Then take the young woman who loses her fiancée to war or a terrible disease. She will go on to become stronger than she ever was, due to that event.

Imagine losing what you think is the love of your life. All the dreams of the future are shattered. Life feels hopeless. Yet by going through this heart-wrenching experience, she is able to reach even higher levels of happiness and joy. She learns to be self-sufficient. She learns to love again, a deeper and more all-encompassing love as well.

Only by having the earlier experience is this improvement, or higher level, in her life able to be attained.

We must all remember God's Righteousness and learn to accept it and, in fact, look forward to it. We also need to remember that God's grace will only take us to the places that he knows we can handle. For we can handle much more than we may think or believe with God's great grace. For He is Righteous and True and knows what's best for us.

Lesson 66 - Loving

The next lesson is on Loving.

Loving each other; Loving All That Is; Loving our Earth, our Universe, our environment, all the creatures and even the little annoying bugs and such.

We are by nature Loving beings; however, sometimes we tend to forget this and tend to have poor attitudes. Attitudes that are ego-based and selfish. We focus too much on ourselves and not on the wonderment of our playground and all that surrounds us.

Instead, we need to "put on a happy face" or change our mindset. Learn to be Loving to others. This can be established in many ways. We will explain a few.

Look within to discover why you're not Loving.

What is lacking in yourself that prevents you from being the Loving creature God created? Are you sad? Lonely? Depressed? Or generally a negative person?

If so, put your chin up and resolve to be more positive and first love yourself.

Remember, you are perfect just as you are!

God is all-knowing and He created you. If God created you as a perfect being, then who are *you* to doubt His creation?

Put a smile on your face and love in your heart (actually, just let it out). Once it has infiltrated your body and soul, spread your love to others.

If you are timid, just offer your smile. If you are a bit shy, just say "Hello" and smile. As you learn to be more Loving, practice Loving deeds to others. Lift them up. Hug them. Appreciate them. Care for them. Pray for them.

These are Loving actions you can learn to do, even if you start from a place of darkness.

Follow these same steps in your treatment of all living creatures, from your pets to wild animals and even little bugs, for they are all created by God to be perfect, just as you are. Learn to embrace them, be Loving towards them, and treat them with the care they deserve.

Especially love those that are hurt or angry for they are both hurting, just for different reasons.

Your enemy holds hurt in his heart and is only lashing out at you. The physical hurt is the same, but you are more able to see their "hurt" whether it's an illness or physical malady. Embrace them for they need your love. You can teach others great love for themselves when you love them even when they are hurt or don't treat you kindly.

This is a lesson God wants us all to learn.

Be Loving to others, all the time, for we all need to *give* and *receive* love if we are to learn and grow as God desires. A necessary step for Ascension, to be sure.

Lesson 66 - Loving

Lesson 67 · **Abundance**

Abundance is a concept all humans must endeavor to grasp, learn, and accommodate.

It simply means there is enough.

God has provided enough. His miraculous planning shows us there is already enough on this great planet to meet all our needs, you just simply have to learn how to access it.

When you feel you are without, it is only your perspective, for you are never without. To be able to use or experience something you feel is lacking is a matter of mindset and effort.

If you are feeling unloved, look around you. Observe others. Give them love freely and you will receive love. See? It was there all along, you just had to learn to access it.

The same goes for finding your special loved one or soulmate. They are here all along. It's a matter of accessing or attracting them to you. There are many steps to achieve this great miracle, which we will explain later. Suffice it to say—they are already with you—you only have to learn how to access that great connection.

Food and other resources are in abundance also. However, many see the *lack* of such things, so their focus is on *lack*, not *Abundance*.

Changing one's focus will get you what you want.

How does one change their focus while in dire situations, you wonder, such as starving tribes in Africa or even malnourished children in developed countries?

We will explain. Take the malnourished child in a supposedly well-to-do community or country. His parents seem to be lacking in the basic knowledge of caring for their child. Perhaps they have no money, due to no job. But there are ways. There are paths out of their poverty. That is what they are here to learn.

Perhaps they must learn to reach out and ask for aid or food gifts from the local community.

Perhaps it is a way to encourage them to visit a food bank or local church pantry.

In that way, it could change the entire trajectory of their lives. Think of it: entire families coming to know the Lord because of a hungry child.

Another scenario is the responsibility this places on the father of the family. Perhaps he has been lackadaisical in providing for his family. Maybe he's lazy or drinks or is unmotivated.

Such dire circumstances may spur him to step up to the plate and make some changes to his life. Try a little harder. Work a little harder. Perhaps become the man, the husband, the father, God intends him to be. There are always ways to find work or even barter for food. An example is to work for a farmer in exchange for food for his family.

Answers are there.

God has already provided.

This is a lesson, a way of life, that we all must learn while we are here.

What do we do when we don't know what to do?

What do we do when we need something desperately for our survival and cannot seem to access it?

Pray, dear child, pray. For then, and only then, will God and his Archangels show you the way.

We all get weary at times and need assistance. There is no crime in asking for help, even though some with strong or big egos may think that way. Even asking God for help is a lesson we must all learn. We need to come to realize that God is all-powerful and He and only He can provide all our needs.

We must *ask* though.

We must learn to set our ego aside and come to Him with an open heart, one full of love for him and All That Is.

Eventually, our egos will subside, and all mankind will live and breathe and make decisions with a heart full of love, not from a place of ego and selfishness. This too is a great, great lesson we are all here to learn and it is one required for Ascension of mankind. We will explain this concept later in more detail too.

Now, on to the topic of creating or finding Abundance in one's everyday life.

We must set our *intention* and *ask*. Then we must *believe* and *wait*. All this is done with an already *grateful* heart.

All is accomplished in God's ever-perfect timing. You see, all is already here, already connected to you and all of us; it is only a matter of realizing or accessing it.

Let's say you want a certain house on a hill, over-looking a valley. It's beautiful beyond anything you've ever seen. You can imagine living there with your family. It would make you feel like a king to provide such a home for your children and later, your grandchildren.

But alas, you have no funds or at least funds of that nature as would be required to purchase it. And there is a family happily residing in the home.

Should you set your intention on this desire, God and the Universe will transpire to bring it to you. It may take years, or it may be quicker in human time; but it will occur if you ask, believe, and wait, along with a grateful heart for the many blessings you already have.

This sort of a "miracle" occurs quite frequently.

It's known as "manifesting."

Many books explain it in detail as do many followers. It's quite easy to do and one that eventually all mankind will learn to accomplish.

The reason we can seemingly create whatever we want is because it already exists. All in our Universe is already connected, we just may not see it or experience it until we "access" it.

This is how and why the great Abundance provided by God already exists. This may be a somewhat lofty goal of understanding for many of us, but we should strive to understand it.

For knowing we already have whatever we need or want can bring about a tremendous amount of peace to our lives here on Earth.

It's a concept God wants us to understand and use to our benefit, for it is a way to bring happiness and joy to our everyday life.

It is a way to experience the very glory of our existence here on Earth.

It is a lesson God wants us all to learn and absorb into our souls: "There is already enough here on Earth to meet our every need and desire."

Lesson 68 - Gratefulness

Next lesson is on Gratefulness.

We all need to learn to be grateful for our many blessings and even those situations where it may seem not to be a blessing.

Ever hear the saying, "It was a blessing in disguise?" Life is very much that way.

Something terrible or even horrific occurs and later we see it was really a blessing. Some examples could be a job loss (even a firing) and later a new and better opportunity comes around.

The ending of a relationship or marriage can be much the same. Once you must redirect your life, you will meet others and have a better relationship. Perhaps and most likely, you've grown from the first relationship and therefore bring growth and insights into the next relationship. Such is our growth process here on Earth.

We are to embrace these lessons and become grateful for them, for this is the way God teaches us.

This is the way we grow.

And these lessons will lead us towards Ascension, which is man's goal while here on Earth.

Even in times of misery and doubt there is always something to be grateful for: the sunshine, a baby's smile, a new flower peeking through the damp soil.

There is *always* something to be grateful for.

It is your mindset that must be changed or adjusted if you fail to see even the tiniest thing (or miracle actually) for which to be grateful.

You are breathing, right? Then thank God for the air you are breathing.

There is a roof over your head, is there not? Even if it's a shabby home or a freeway overpass, you do have a roof over your head. So be thankful. Be grateful. Thank God for your blessings.

You see, those who are happy and thank God for their blessings will continue to have more blessings bestowed on them.

Those humans who bitterly complain about the lack of their desires will continue to have lack.

Mindset is the difference. Your mindset will attract what you focus on. There are metaphysical reasons this occurs, but most humans are more concerned about *whether or not* this works, not *how* it works.

Suffice it to say, you can have, be or do anything you want in life. Part of the process is being grateful for what you already have.

Failure to be grateful, i.e. being stubborn and close-minded, will reap you more of what you have: *lack*!

Doesn't Gratefulness seem like a much better path? This is the path God wants us to take.

Lesson 69 - Compassion

Compassion is a topic we should all strive to learn more about.

The importance of compassion cannot be underrated.

Our natural state is love and kindness. When we are unable to deal with life, those characteristics tend to disappear. But when we remain happy, cheerful, and content, we are usually overflowing with Compassion for our self and others.

This is as God intends.

You see, when we are content with ourselves, we think and care more about others. When we are not and become self-absorbed within our own ego, we haven't the ability to care for others.

It's really important to put aside our ego and self-concentration and *think* more about others.

Think about what we can do to help them.

Think about how we can bring joy to their lives.

In turn, we will see our own discontent fade away. By helping them, we lift ourselves up.

This is another one of God's perfect miracles, designed to encourage us to grow and learn as we travel the path to our higher selves.

Do not forget the lesson of Compassion, for it will serve us all well. It is the quickest way to improve your inner self.

Lesson 70 - Turmoil

Turmoil and doubt are designed as turning points in our life.

When we reach this, we have to dig deep and figure out what we are made of. Will we rise above the situation and accompanying feelings, or will we succumb to it?

Either path is acceptable.

It's just that one path is more circuitous and therefore takes longer.

Do not ever be afraid of making a mistake, for there is no such thing as a mistake. It's all a learning experience. You do not get brownie points at Heaven's Gate when you arrive, you just might arrive a little more quickly.

So, when life presents you a tumultuous circumstance, you must learn to push doubt (your self-doubt and those doubting friends) out of your consciousness.

Know that God has your best interests at heart and step ahead boldly with confidence to handle the situation. *For with God and your best effort, anything is truly possible.*

Step out of the fear into greatness.

Put the Turmoil behind you to the best of your abilities and move on. You will not only prove to yourself that you can do so, but you will serve as a mighty example to others, for they are always watching and observing others.

You may never know how many others you influence by your bold and courageous actions. Even if all you ever feel is a sense of accomplishment and self-worth for conquering your own fears and moving ahead, it will be a great lesson to you and a wonderful confidence-booster.

This is as God intended. He wants you to feel powerful, brave, courageous, and bold. It is a pre-cursor to knowing—and truly believing—just how capable we as human beings are and can be.

There is great strength in numbers. As more and more humans learn to step out of fear and doubt and make bold decisions, our entire planet will advance in boldness and seek to become the kind of human nation God intends, all moving ahead as one great entity—mankind.

This will happen eventually; we have no doubt. The timing is dependent on when mankind takes these steps forward.

Each person's actions, no matter how small, affect another's. This is how mankind will move forward to a happy and more joyous planet. One step at a time.

Let us all do our part.

Lesson 71 · Happiness — Why?

Today's lesson is on Happiness — why we should be happy and why God wants us to be happy.

The feelings inside us can be happy, sad, or ambivalent. Our natural nature is to be happy, joyful, and loving, yet at times we feel unhappy or sad.

There is a reason for this, namely that if we were happy all the time, we would never know sadness. In order to fully appreciate Happiness, one must have felt or experienced sadness.

It's the dichotomy or duality one must experience in all things: the "with" and the "without." For once we feel the difference, we can more fully appreciate the other experience.

If we were always happy, we wouldn't know sadness.

If we never learned or felt sadness, we not only wouldn't appreciate the happy times, but there would be no lessons to learn. No lessons, then no growth. So you can see now how all this is intertwined to expedite our learning process here on Earth.

This is another example of God's miracles in planning and creating our wonderful universe—our playground as it were—for it is the most wonderful of classrooms to enjoy the experience of being a human.

We are most appreciative of God's vision and should *all* endeavor to learn the many lessons herein provided that will lead not one, but all to a better existence through our joint Ascension.

Being happy and learning how to be happy is an important part of Ascension. Let us explain how one goes about becoming happy.

It is all a matter of mindset actually. A method we can easily train ourselves in if we are diligent and pay attention to how it all works.

If we accept the fact that God has already provided our every need through His great abundance, then there is no need to feel lack.

If there is no lack, then there is no need to feel sad or unhappy.

One just needs to learn how to access the abundance as discussed in a previous chapter.

The other action we must take in order to be happy is to remove or push aside doubt. Doubt is nothing more than negative thinking rearing its ugly head. Cast your doubts aside, as well as those supposedly well-meaning comments from others that are really negative thoughts designed to plant doubt in your consciousness.

If your mindset remains positive, you will be happy.

These are actions we must all learn here on Earth, for our Happiness is truly within our power. A great and worthy lesson for us to learn and follow.

We can also help others achieve Happiness not only by discussing and explaining it to them, but by our many actions.

When someone sees or observes us being happy, they wonder, "How does she do that?" or "What's she so happy about?"

It is wonderful to serve as a shining example to others of being happy. It shows them it is possible. It shows them that others can overcome doubts and negative situations and still be happy.

Never underestimate the effect your Happiness has on others. We can all do this. If you don't want to be happy for yourself, be happy for others, for it is contagious—a feeling you can easily "catch" from another.

Have you ever noticed when you are around a happy-go-lucky person and you leave them feeling more joyous and positive yourself? That is how it all works. That is an example of how connected we all are, too.

Like we explained before, God has designed a wonderful playground in which we are to learn these many lessons, the least of which is Happiness.

One last note: even though others can "catch" our Happiness if they are open and observant, no one is responsible for another person's Happiness.

We can serve as an example or a teacher, as it were, but everyone is responsible for their own Happiness. For if they were not, how would they learn? How would they grow? We can teach others, but they have to do the work.

Unfortunately, many humans feel someone "owes" them a happy life. This is not the case at all! *They* are responsible for determining what makes them happy and how to go about achieving it. Such a process is well within each of our capabilities. We must learn how to take the necessary steps and become happy.

Being happy is not just accepting how things are, especially in difficult times; it is also a matter of creating our own Happiness. But in order to create our own Happiness, we must discover—or uncover—what truly makes us happy.

This process itself teaches us many lessons, most commonly that money or things do not provide lasting Happiness.

Lasting Happiness is found *within*, in a contented soul, one that has learned many lessons—least of all, how to be happy, truly happy.

One day, all mankind will learn how to be happy.

It's something for all of us to learn and show others. Happiness, true Happiness, will undoubtedly aid mankind on our joint Ascension as God has planned.

Let's each do our part to lead mankind in that direction.

Lesson 72 - Difficulties and Ramifications

Difficulties and Ramifications are other lessons to learn.

When situations occur and various Difficulties are encountered, this can be a time for great growth in our lives. This is the time to draw on our many skills and forge ahead to overcome these unpleasantries.

Difficulties or trials are merely little tests designed to spur growth inside us—or among us if it's a group difficulty. As mentioned previously throughout this discourse, we should be thankful for the difficult times as they will likely lead to our greatest growth. Even if *great* growth is not attained, there will be growth.

Ramifications are quite another thing. When we go through our different seasons, the choices we make and the subsequent actions we take will have certain Ramifications or results. These results shape our future or the future of others.

We must be conscious of and considerate of these Ramifications when we are deciding how to deal with the various Difficulties we encounter in life.

Sometimes we might discover a quick fix for us on an issue; however, the Ramifications to another person or another living creature in the Universe is profound and therefore must be reconsidered. Since we are all connected—all living entities in the Universe—this can be quite a complex undertaking.

To reiterate a quote sometimes heard: "It's not all about us." This is something to keep in mind when making decisions and solving problems. It's not all about us and what *we* want. There are other consequences to consider.

God wants us to be aware of our connectedness to the rest of the Universe so we can make better choices. It's a way we can learn to be more mindful and responsible for our actions. For our actions truly do not merely affect just us.

We are "One" and thus truly connected to All That Is. Even simple choices can have immense effects in the long-term.

Just be aware of these consequences and do your best, as that is what God requires from us.

Lesson 73 ⁃ Compassion and Feelings

Today's lesson is on Compassion.

Compassion is what we *feel* for others in their times of need, whether it be a physical need, an emotional need, or a spiritual need.

You see, since we are all connected, we can *feel* these strong emotions when others have them. It's one of God's little miracles to show us and teach us and even remind us that we are all connected—truly, deeply connected—all the way to our soul level.

Those of the same soul clan or soul family are even more so "in tune" with each other. Nonetheless, all mankind is connected at some level.

When we see a starving child in Africa or the back woods of Kentucky, we want to help them. We want to nurture them and feed them. These are the feelings that come with Compassion.

We all *have* these feelings.

Whether we *act* on these feelings is quite another matter.

God would prefer we *do* act on these feelings.

The first logical step, He would hope, is that you'd acknowledge your feelings in such a situation. Allowing those feelings to permeate through you, and into your soul, allows you to be more connected to others. It's quite a natural thing to do, for that is how we were designed by God.

These deep feelings are not to be simply put to rest. No, God would hope that such feelings would spur one into action.

Do something to aid another's situation. Help them yourself. Donate to a worthy group who would help them. Give of your own time to help. When all else fails, pray, and pray sincerely and deeply for them. Prayers do work, but most of all it shows God you are Compassionate and willing to do your part to ease the suffering.

Doing your best in any given situation is all that God requires.

Are you beginning to see the importance of Compassion?

Do you see how it is intertwined with our connectedness?

Do you see why God developed Compassion as a means to our growth?

It's an important lesson to learn. It's a way we can show God's love to others. God works through us to do great acts. So you are actually being designed by God to help God accomplish great things.

You are capable of greatness yourself therefore, but Compassion for others comes first. It's a first step in

starting on the path to true enlightenment or becoming—
or attaining—your higher self.

Lesson 74 · Consciousness — Different Levels

The lesson today is on Consciousness.

What exactly is Consciousness, you may ask. Let us explain.

First of all, there are different levels of Consciousness, which in itself may be a somewhat difficult concept to understand.

There is our subconscious mind which is always at work—thinking and planning and scheming—even when we are asleep. Some people may not be aware of the importance of our subconscious mind.

It's important because it all starts here in each and every one of us. We are often not even aware of our subconscious, but they exist, nonetheless.

When someone is mean to you, you may have a subconscious thought of how you dislike them, even though you might not admit it. The thought exists inside your mind, but exists, nonetheless. Later your unconscious thought may cause you to act out in such a way or say something out loud because of your subconscious thought.

It is much like this:

Subconscious → Conscious → Physical Act

It all starts in the subconscious, where you aren't even aware that it affects the outcome in physical reality.

Next, let's talk about the conscious mind. That one we are all aware of.

We think thoughts which consciously lead us to act—or not act—in our physical world. We're all aware of our conscious thoughts.

But did you know you can control your conscious thoughts? Yes, you can! One can even control their unconscious thoughts.

There are methods to do both which lead us to a happier, healthier, and more mindful life—one we should all strive to live. Such a life God intends for us to learn how to live while we are here on Earth.

In fact, learning to control our actions through controlling our thoughts (both conscious and unconscious) is exactly what God wants us to learn!

This may seem like an overwhelming or possibly a scary or unrealistic proposition, but we can assure you, it is not. We are *all* quite capable of learning to do so.

The first step is being aware how our thoughts—conscious *and* subconscious—do indeed affect our actions.

The next step is creating the proper thoughts or planting the thoughts we would *like* into our conscious and subconscious minds.

Let us explain by an example. A young woman looks in the mirror, naked, in the morning She sees an overweight girl, flabby skin, chubby face, crooked teeth, no smile, messy hair and her subconscious mind tells her she's ugly. This negative thought has been there so long that it has become part of her conscious thought process. She not only thinks she's ugly, she will say it out loud! She's unhappy about it, but she just says it like a declaration, "I am Ugly."

We all know what connotations go along with such words: unworthiness, unlovable, unimportant, and certainly feeling she has no value. But this is not true. She is merely letting her thoughts control the eventual outcome she feels about herself.

What if she told herself that she was beautiful?

What if she wrote a little affirmation that said, "I am beautiful, I am perfect, God created me; therefore, I am perfect just as I am?"

Once this was repeated regularly, she would start to smile. She would hold her head up high and her posture would improve. Her eyes would be bright. She would interact with others more easily. They would complement her. She'd start to feel better about herself. She might even eat less and exercise more, lending itself to improvements in her physical being.

Soon she would have confidence and eventually, when she stood naked in front of the mirror, she'd say, "I am beautiful. I am happy. I am perfect just as God created me" …and she would mean it!

Quite a difference, right? And it's all because she fed her mind good thoughts about herself.

The same process happens to a child because we are quite shaped by our surroundings and early treatment when we are young. We are learning as a species that how parents and teachers and other adults treat children early on has quite an effect on their self-image.

They—as children—may not know what to think about themselves, so they absorb what others say about them or how they treat them. If they are met with a constant barrage of comments such as "You're stupid" or "You'll never learn" or treatment that makes them feel unworthy (no hugs, lack of food and/or attention) they will come to feel unworthy and stupid.

If, however, they are met with a constant barrage of compliments, they will shine and grow. Their frowns will turn to smiles, the light in their eyes will shine, they will be happy and inquisitive versus shy and withdrawn. Quite a difference indeed.

In a sense, we all start out as children, perhaps in a somewhat negative situation or at least in a place where we feel lost or uncertain about ourselves. Our life experiences shape us.

But once we are older and become more aware of our life and how *we* can influence our life and have more control over it, it is our duty (or our job) to discover or uncover how to be happier within ourselves so we lead a more joyful life.

It becomes our responsibility to learn how to shape our internal thoughts (both subconscious and unconscious) to lead us where we want to go: on to the path of a conscious self-directed and full life.

It is our promise to God to do so and continue to do the very best we can. Do not take this promise lightly, for with our promises, God has given us all the power to do so. The power to shape our very lives through our thoughts and therefore our actions. These are very powerful abilities, ones that should not be squandered on unworthy causes.

Think of it this way: if you had unlimited powers (which you do) would you waste it on frivolous actions, or would you strive for greatness?

Would you strive for all you could be?

Would you strive to assist all mankind to be all that we as a collective species can be?

Would you use your gifts, your abilities, and your powers to the best of your abilities? This is what God desires from us. This is the responsibility we all have. Whether we do so is up to each of us in this lifetime.

If we choose to waste our gifts and remain in the lower levels of Consciousness, never reaching our pinnacle, then we will undoubtedly return for another lifetime of lessons. Once we learn the lessons and harness the power of our unconscious mind and conscious mind, we will live as God intended and serve as an example to others, in turn lifting them up.

In such a scenario, eventually all mankind will live in a state of higher Consciousness, one in which he is more aware of himself, others, and the interconnectedness of All That Is. Because remember: we are all One. One cohesive inter-connected entity.

We are all God in a sense because there is no division between us. A difficult concept to be sure, one that will be discussed later for a more complete understanding.

Suffice it to say, we are here to learn to control our subconscious—and therefore our conscious—thought which will lead us to a higher level of Consciousness where we are more aware of our existence and hence our connectedness to All.

Lesson 75 · Commitment

Today's lesson is on Commitments — the ones we have with each other and the ones we hold with God or our Spiritual Leader.

It's important to keep our Commitments. It's a covenant with God and a promise to others. Failure to do so lessens the connections to others. They see you in a different light. They know they cannot count on you.

When a man marries, he has a Commitment to his wife and any children born. (Even if it is unsaid, it still exists.) For God commands such behavior when we take another in Holy Matrimony.

All marriages are considered a holy Commitment even if not performed in a church. This is truly a sacred Commitment to care for each other all the days of your lives here on Earth.

God created marriage so man would strive for the best and fulfill his and her Commitments. Sometimes it doesn't work out, but it is as God plans, nevertheless.

The lessons were to be learned as can only occur in the sanction of marriage. Sometimes people die or divorce. They move on for various reasons.

The important part is to learn the lessons presented and grow into better beings. Sometimes we do not learn the lessons and have to repeat the same unhappy lessons in a marriage to another. All the more important to *pay attention* so as to avoid the continued or repeated unhappiness.

In a loving and kind marriage, there are many lessons one can learn. In fact, it is a wonderful way in which to experience great growth. However, it works best if both partners are willing to grow.

Let's take an example. The husband does not step up and do his part to care for his family both financially and emotionally. The wife senses something is missing. This is because she's fearful the financial needs of her family won't be met. She consequently loses confidence and faith in her man's abilities. He then loses confidence in himself.

A brave and determined man will dig deep within and perhaps ask God for help if he's not too prideful. He will change. He will grow. He will do whatever is necessary to financially provide for his family.

A woman can sense and know all this. Sometimes she realizes her man is incompetent in his role and will move on. She has learned to identify the failure of a marriage: lack of trust and confidence in your mate.

Another woman may stay with her incompetent mate despite unhappiness. She tries to stay upbeat and happy, nonetheless. It doesn't work. Her man still fails to step up to his natural place in the family. She learns to "be the man" as it were to assume the financial role of the family. Her heart strings grow. She loves her man despite his actions. She learns and grows despite the hardships.

So either way, we all learn and grow, which is as God desires.

Let's take the act of commitment with others in another scenario. We make a plan to meet another at a certain time, yet we are tardy or do not attend. What does the other person think: we are forgetful, they aren't important, or we just don't meet our Commitments? Failure to meet one's Commitments is a failing of one's character.

It's easy to keep one's Commitments if you follow one simple rule: don't make a Commitment if you don't intend to keep it!

Be honest about your desires, even if you feel pressured by another. Never make a Commitment unless your heart and soul are in it, even if it's a small Commitment. It is simply not necessary. Find another way to convey this when speaking to another or just tell them "no." It's better to be honest than mislead another with a Commitment you don't intend to keep.

This is important not only adult to adult, but very much so when dealing with children, for they observe the Commitments adults make to each other which re-enforces how they think one makes and keeps (or doesn't keep) their Commitments.

Take for example a child who hears his father tell his mother they will take a little trip next month. The child is all excited, very much looking forward to the trip. When it doesn't happen, his hopes are dashed. He doubts his father's word. When his mother doesn't hold the father accountable, he learns there are no consequences for failing to meet one's Commitments. He learns this is acceptable behavior, one that he may carry out in his own life.

See how Commitments and failure to keep Commitments affect our feelings and actions towards others?

Do you understand the importance of keeping one's Commitments?

Now, let's talk or explain about Commitments to God.

Before we start each earthly journey, we make certain Commitments to God called covenants. These are holy promises that we intend to complete while on our specific journey or visit. Failure to do so will certainly bring God's wrath upon us.

This may seem harsh, but God promises us great things in return for our Commitments so it's very important to follow through, despite the hardships and despite the costs. For God has given us all that is necessary to fulfill those same Commitments. The only thing we must provide is the willingness to follow through.

It is only our determination and *trying* that separates us from fulfilling our Commitments or not. In the big scheme of life it is only our best effort that God demands, and we must give it, so it's actually a very small price on our part that is required for all the greatness God has provided.

Lesson 75 - Commitment

Lesson 76 - Responsibility

Today's discourse is on Responsibility.

We each have a certain Responsibility to ourselves, each other and to God.

Let us explain. For ourselves, it is our Responsibility (or job) while we are here on Earth to learn and grow and to understand the many lessons God has set forth for us. Such learning is our Responsibility and our Responsibility alone. Others may help, prod, or teach us, but it is up to us to do the actual work involved.

We also have a certain level of Responsibility or commitment to assist others on their journey to Ascension, for we are all connected. One person's Ascension helps another and vice versa. It's like helping a teammate: it is to be expected. We are all on the same team—a team or tribe of all mankind—not just the people in your local community.

All beings hold this Responsibility to help each other and to learn and grow while here.

This is a covenant with God before we arrive here on Earth. It is one of the promises we made to God prior to our arrival and not a promise to be taken lightly.

We all have the Responsibility to honor this commitment and do our very best, for that and that alone is all that God requires. Doing our best means doing our best to grow individually and in conjunction with others. This is a deep and serious Responsibility, one not to be taken lightly.

There are other types of Responsibilities, too, that result from the formation of a family unit.

Once married, a man has a sacred Responsibility to care for his wife and any children born or adopted into that marriage. Such Responsibility cannot and will not be dissolved in the event the marriage is dissolved or comes to an end. The Responsibility to care for the wife and children continues throughout one's lifetime on Earth. This too, is not a Responsibility to be taken lightly.

The woman on the other hand has quite different Responsibilities once married. Her main goal is to nurture and love her husband and children. While the man's Responsibilities are mostly financial, the woman's Responsibility is mainly nurturing—making all in her family feel loved and important. She does this by seeing to their needs. Needs such as food and caring for them emotionally and physically. A bit like a nursemaid, doctor, and cook, all in one.

Such is a huge Responsibility and very important in the development of mankind, for where would we all be without the nurturing love of our dear mothers? To be a mother and carry out one's Responsibilities well is truly an act of selfless love. God knows this and he respects the woman's commitment to do a good and holy job, for he knows the future of all mankind hinges on the role of mothers.

Back to the father for a moment. The role of the father is not to be undervalued either, for they are the Responsible leader of the household. They alone are Responsible for the financial means of the family. It is their Responsibility to learn, how to create the financial security necessary to provide for their family. A wife has sufficient Responsibilities on her own without having to take over the man's financial Responsibility too.

It would be wise for young women to remember this when selecting a husband. Will he take Responsibility for his family? Does he care for her sufficiently to do so? Is he capable of providing her a suitable life?

This introspection would help immensely with the formation of future family units, for if a woman was truthful with herself and the capabilities of her possible mate, she would avoid selecting one of poor qualities who is not yet capable of providing for a family.

This is not to say such marriages are a mistake, for they too will lead to lessons. But if a woman seeks a "short cut," as it were, then these questions would be most helpful. Such choices also tend to spur the man along because he sees he cannot have a wife he wants until he grows and is ready to accept his part of the Responsibility of marriage.

When both partners know and accept the Responsibility of marriage, they have a better chance for a long and happy marriage.

Remember: marriage in itself is a sacred contract with the man, the woman, and God.

It is known as the Sacred Union, the most holy of unions here on Earth (with the exception of one's relationship with God, Source or whatever one's chosen spiritual leader is).

Lesson 77 · Sacred Union

Sacred Union – what is it and what does it truly mean? What does such a union encompass and why is it "Sacred?" These questions and more will be addressed here.

When a man and a woman give each other freely in Holy Matrimony—as it is called in God's religion (it's referred to a bit differently in other religions, but the requirements are the same) —the man is assuming financial responsibility for the woman and any children they may have. This is a binding contract with God even if the marriage dissolves through death, divorce, or other separation. The man will be held to this responsibility all the days of his earthly life.

The man also promises and is expected to care for the wife in a loving and caring way so as to meet her needs for a male companion. This involves listening to her, performing acts of kindness, and loving her deeply. Growing in his love for her, till it becomes deep and true.

This is one of the lessons marriage teaches us: to love deeply and without limits. In the earthly realm, it is called unconditional love. This is the type of love God wants us to experience. This is the type of love that requires sacrifice, which God wants us to learn about. It's part of our growth process.

The woman on the other hand, has quite different responsibilities in the context of a Sacred Marriage or Sacred Union. Her role is to obey her man—and by that we don't mean to blindly follow him and put up with abuse—we mean to have the confidence in him and his abilities to perform his duties as the head of the household.

You see, the husband draws his strength from his wife's perception of him. If she sees him as an able provider, he will become one. If she thinks he's weak and cannot provide, he will fill that bill instead.

This is not to say a woman's lack of confidence in her man is her fault when he fails to perform—for the final actions of any of us is dependent on *us*—it just means that a woman's feeling or perception or belief in her man plays an important part in his success.

The man is responsible for providing the financial means to care for the family so the woman can concentrate on her part—the nurturing and caring for other needs, such as food and a comfortable home.

Both jobs and responsibilities are equally important. Both sets of responsibilities must be carried out for a happy, joyous, and productive home. We all need to strive for such a perfect union in our relationship within marriage. Few have obtained it so far, but it is attainable, and all should continue to strive for it.

You see, God intended for Sacred Unions to be our most holy of unions here on Earth so we could learn to grow in our love for one another, much like He wants us to grow in our love for Him.

This is the vehicle He so perfectly designed; to teach us many lessons and so we could each experience true, deep, and caring love—love that transcends all boundaries.

For someday, we as beings will all experience such deep and true love for *all* beings.

The relationship within Holy Matrimony starts our human development on this worthy path.

Such is the plan of God—a most glorious plan—one in which we are each on the path to fulfilling for His and our benefits.

Lesson 77 · Sacred Union

*Lesson 78 - Wonderment and Joy

The Earth is full of Wonderment and Joy.

Do not let these opportunities pass you by, for God created them for your enjoyment.

Notice the word "Joy" within the word enjoyment? We are to constantly seek Joy. We are to constantly be in wonder of our awesome playground of learning.

You see, with all work and no Wonderment and Joy, we might become disillusioned and give up on our quest to learn and grow.

God has perfectly placed much Joy and Wonderment in our everyday life: the flowers, the trees, the mountains, and the sunshine. The rising sun and the setting sun. The birds and the bees and our dear children. We should live in awe of all these wonderful creations.

When we learn the hard lessons—the difficult lessons, the lessons filled with deep sorrow—we can look around and see our world has not fallen apart.

There is still Joy.

There is still beauty.

And we can be in a state of wonder of all that it is—all that God created for us.

For He wants us to remain grounded in His word, His promises and as such has provided our beautiful playground as a backdrop to our learning.

Do not forget the Wonderment of life here on Earth in your bad times, for good times will follow. All you have to do is open your eyes and see it all around you, like a comforting hug from the Almighty.

Go about your day today. Absorb the lessons. Learn and grow. And observe and be thankful for the wonderful creation surrounding you.

Be in Wonder!

Experience the Joy!

Let it be absorbed into your soul, no matter the troubles you may be experiencing, for they too will pass.

Let the Wonder and Joy engulf you on your journey and provide you the comfort that God so desires. Be one with All That Is and your troubles will fade and disappear.

Lesson 79 - Conceit

Conceit is a feeling experienced by many so let us discuss it here.

Conceit is when one is full of himself and puts himself above others. He thinks he is perfect. He thinks he doesn't have to follow the rules. He thinks he's better than others and treats them so. In fact, he may ignore them as unworthy beings.

This is not how God would want us to act, be and live. We are all equal in God's eyes. We are all important in God's eyes.

We are all here for a purpose.

It is not our job to judge others and place ourselves above them.

God would much prefer we treat all humans (and even animals and our environment) with the respect they deserve.

To be Conceited robs us of the joy of interacting with those we wrongfully place below us. For how are we to learn if we have no interaction with a large part of the population? We would be missing out on the many lessons they could teach us. We could miss out on the opportunity to grow and become all we can be. In this scenario, we are not following our promise to God to learn and grow because we aren't even in the classroom to observe the lessons.

"Well, you might think, what can *I* learn from a poor, uneducated peon so far below me that I can barely notice them?" Plenty to be sure!

First of all, you could learn compassion. Compassion for others less fortunate than you, for those who are hungry, or live in humble abodes (or maybe no abodes).

You could observe how they find joy in life despite their circumstances.

You could realize the material belongings you possess do not necessarily make you happier, for many beneath you are quite happy with their circumstances in life.

The dichotomy of your life and the lives of others helps you recognize how your life could have been without actually experiencing it. You will become more appreciative of your life.

There are many lessons to learn from others in different circumstances: humility, contentment, graciousness, and love are just a few.

Being Conceited keeps one from observing and learning the lessons we are here to learn.

Conceited people tend to be judgmental. Judging of others is not our place for it is reserved for God alone. We are here to help lift each other up, not judge them because we think they haven't progressed as well as they should have.

Lastly, think about how *you* would feel or have felt when others have judged you by *their* Conceited actions. You did not feel pleasant, right?

Perhaps you shrugged off their treatment.

Perhaps it hurt you deeply and took years to overcome.

Perhaps you are *still* struggling.

Conceit and maltreatment of others resulting from judging can create a negative cycle of behavior among humans. God wants us to learn and grow sufficiently so as these behaviors are no longer accepted or followed. He wants us to grow past such behaviors.

In fact, we must learn not to be Conceitful or judgmental if mankind is to ascend. It is most certainly a lesson we are here to learn.

Lesson 80 ~ Hatred

Hatred is another action/feeling we must all learn to absolve ourselves from while on our journey here on Earth.

There is no benefit to Hatred unless it is to see the damage it can inflict.

We should instead endeavor to understand those that we hate. Perhaps if we met them with a heart full of understanding and love, the Hatred would disappear.

Let's take an example: you are filled with hate for another person. The reason you have adopted this attitude could be fueled by rumors or statements from others. They might even be unfounded charges.

You are incensed, filled with hate and anger, yet you are thinking and looking at the situation only from one view.

Perhaps the culprit has another side. Maybe there are circumstances you aren't aware of; circumstances so horrendous you couldn't even imagine. If you knew these circumstances perhaps your Hatred wouldn't be so strong.

Perhaps your Hatred would even dissolve. Possibly even dissolve into compassion and understanding for the other's plight.

Perhaps even one day your compassion would turn to love for this person. This is all possible through understanding.

But one must be open to understanding for it to occur. This takes an open mind and an open heart. It requires us to put our pre-conceived notions aside and be willing to listen and learn.

Hatred, of course, is not how God wants us to live. He wants us to embrace each other and live in a place of peace and harmony. Hatred has no place in this scenario.

It is our calling to do whatever we can to reduce Hatred among mankind for Hatred only divides us. Remember we are all One and we should endeavor to act and behave as such.

When we observe others living in Hatred or exhibiting Hatred, it is our duty to speak up. We don't need to be bossy and overruling to them. There are other ways, possibly through suggestions.

One can say things like, "It might not be as is commonly known. Things aren't always as they seem. Perhaps there is more to the story than our one-sided view."

Or even be so bold as to remind them that God wants us to love our enemies.

Even a small discussion will help to eventually change mankind's mind about Hatred.

Someday Hatred will no longer exist in our world. Then we will be ready for Ascension as a co-mingled consciousness.

Until that time comes, we all need to do our part to eliminate Hatred.

Lesson 80 · Hatred

Lesson 81 ⋅ Destiny

We all have a great Destiny as is already set forth by God.

Whether we reach our final Destiny each lifetime is up to us though.

It requires effort.

It requires learning.

It requires passion beyond what one usually experiences during a lifetime. It is a compelling desire that will lift one to their greatest Destiny, their pinnacle of attainment here on Earth.

For you see, God does have great plans for each of us. These plans are set in stone before we even set our very first foot here on Earth.

Which lifetime we achieve our final Destiny in is up to us. As we learn lessons and grow each lifetime, we become more prepared to reach our Destiny.

It requires effort.

It requires stamina.

It requires the ability to push forward despite the costs and despite the odds. It is compelling; like a "knowing" inside that this great thing must be accomplished. We are all quite capable of completing such magic. It's just a matter of when we have prepared ourselves and when we are ready to complete this grand task.

We've all seen great people, maybe not famous, but determined people who will not give up on their chosen goal or destination. These are likely the ones on their final mission here on Earth, for they are determined indeed.

Another way to observe and know which ones are working on their final mission is whether their goal will affect the human race and move it or the planet further ahead.

Will their mission or goal have an effect on the rest of the world in a positive light?

Will their actions improve the plight of others? (Mother Teresa).

Will their discovery have great meaning to all? (Edison).

Will their vision shape the view of the world? (Elon Musk).

Will their actions cause others to take a serious look at life in another way? (Dali Lama).

We can all be such Masters, and we will be, once we are truly ready to step into greatness.

Such action does require certain lessons be learned. Most notable: perseverance and our connectedness to all. Other traits or abilities include: willingness to follow guidance from God, having faith in themselves, trusting the process, and the desire to succeed at any cost.

The doubts—from others and oneself—must be put aside. One needs to surge ahead despite worries. Be knowledgeable and aware, yet unstoppable.

This is the way to complete your Destiny or your final mission in life.

There is no shame if one is unable to complete the mission, for there are no mistakes and you will be given another chance to succeed. That does not mean we should give up when our efforts seem too difficult. It just means we must give our best effort, for that and that alone is what God requires from us.

Should we do so (give our best effort) and not reach our Destiny, God will give us another chance.

There are no mistakes; there are only lessons along the way.

Do not be fearful my child. For your Destiny has been set before each of us and we are quite capable of achieving it, for we ARE much more powerful than we know or can even imagine.

We are capable of greatness, as our Creator has endowed us with such capabilities. We merely need to learn how to unleash such capabilities to reach our final Destiny (or mission) in this iteration of life here on Earth.

Ask for guidance.

Ask for clarity.

Ask for help and you will be on your way to greatness.

Lesson 82 - Compatibility and Ascension

You may wonder why Compatibility is a lesson required for Ascension.

Let me explain. It all starts in the subconscious, whether we know so or not. Our thoughts become things—physical things. This is one of the great abilities human beings possess.

This is great power and should be harnessed and properly used.

Take an example of a poor man walking on a street. He's using a cane to maneuver through the cobblestone streets, and he is partially blind.

A young boy, say 4 or 5, is kicking a soccer ball down the narrow alleyway between buildings as the old man approaches. He kicks the ball into the man and hits him by mistake.

The old man smiles. For even though he is jolted, once he hears the boy apologize, he realizes what has happened. The feeling of the ball hitting his shins reminds him of a time long ago when he played soccer (or football as it's called in his country).

He remembers the freedom of running down the field, arms flailing, legs moving swiftly, eyes keenly on the ball. His teammates were behind him as he held the lead and wove in and out the opposing team members until he reached the goal posts and proudly kicked the ball in as he adeptly averted the last member of the opposing team. The goalie, being distracted or perhaps by the hand of God, could not stop the ball. The shot went in and his team won the game!

This seemingly insignificant encounter (the young boy and the blind man), actually had great benefits for both of them.

The boy learned to be a bit more observant of how his actions affect others. Remember all he knows is what he observed: that the old man was somewhat jolted or shocked when hit by his ball.

The old man learned to appreciate the boy's enthusiasm and love for soccer even though it was mildly disconcerting, for the memory it ignited was well-worth the momentary shock or stunning of being hit. It helped him step back in time and re-live a glorious time in his childhood, one he had almost forgotten.

You see, the two individuals are quite Compatible: helping one another along the journey of life.

Such is the way all beings should strive to be to each other: teaching each other and providing a background for learning and growth.

This is as God desires. This is the path to Ascension and a lesson we all must learn in order to advance to the next level of human consciousness here on Earth.

Learn it well, my child, for such is the way of mankind, the future of mankind, where all kindred souls unite as One with one singular purpose: growth and advancement leading us back to our one main attribute, Love.

(Editor's Note: This lesson was mostly shown in pictures and then written, versus transcribed in words.)

Lesson 82 - Compatibility and Ascension

Lesson 83 - Resourcefulness

Resourcefulness is the ability to use the existing physical or emotional resources to complete a task or heal a need.

You are being Resourceful when you attempt to build or create a certain item of your desire by making use of existing materials and tools.

We've all tried to *fix* a certain object and magically found just the right piece of wood or item that could be used like a tool and *voila!* it was repaired.

Ever wonder why that happens?

It is merely God's doing because you *asked*. He will set whatever you need in your path, if only you will ask.

Take another scenario: you are downtrodden. The weight of the world is on your shoulders, seemingly. You need hope. You need answers. You clearly need help as your mind is filled with negative thoughts and seemingly insurmountable doubt.

If you continue in this manner, you may succumb to intense sadness and severe physical pain; but if you are Resourceful, things can have quite a different outcome.

If you look around, you can see hope in simple things, like the seedling turned to a tiny sapling. You can see God's beauty in a sunrise. You can feel grateful as you note your blessings. The gifts are there and if you are resourceful and observing, you can find them.

If your mere environment is not sufficient to lift you, then by all means, ask for help.

Ask for hope.

Ask to be filled with gratitude.

Ask to be made whole again so you can cope.

By these methods, God will make you whole again. You'll be able to go about your day with joy and happiness inside your being.

It's all about being Resourceful. This is how we as human beings fill our needs. Do not let God's many blessings go to waste for the blessings—as well as God—are always present. We just need to learn to be Resourceful.

Do not neglect to use your resources to help others.

Being kind and compassionate by sharing resources with others or showing them how to partake of such resources is a valuable contribution to mankind, one that should not be underestimated. For we can all influence the lives of others by being Resourceful and setting an example of how to do so (by using our resources to lift others) and by glorifying God by asking for His resources and giving thanks for them.

This too, is a good act for others to witness, as it helps them to believe in God's greatness and it gives them inner peace and comfort.

Being Resourceful is a divine gift or attribute we all possess and should endeavor to exhibit in our daily lives.

Lesson 84 ~ Timing

All things happen in God's Time, not our time.

When we ask for something, God knows best and will deliver your wishes at the appropriate time, whether you think so or not.

You may wish and pray and cry out loud in vain for your desires, but they or it will only be delivered in God's Timing. You see, God understands all. God knows all. He knows the perfect Timing to deliver your requests.

Sometimes you may even ask for something repeatedly and it doesn't appear or come into your physical realm. That is because God knows it is not what you need and therefore, seemingly denies your request.

But wait and later you will discover why. Perhaps this item you requested is not right for you or perhaps God has something else entirely in mind for you. Do not doubt God's actions, for remember He is all-knowing and sees and understands what you cannot.

Your actions and Timing are another matter. When God or your Archangels tug on your ear or even your heart strings and tell you to do something such as taking even a small action, listen up! They are guiding you to greatness and the Timing is ever so important.

Not following their wisdom will lead you to prolonged pain or bewilderment.

Not doing as requested or suggested will miss precious Timing. Events and consequences will be off, and it may take years for the circumstances to come back into play again.

An example would be in soap operas where two lovers fail to state their intentions or feelings to one another and then scenes shift and other activities occur. The Timing is lost, and their lives take another direction. You see how their lost opportunity for declaring their love led them down another path on another journey.

Such is our lives here on Earth. Do try not to let such opportunities pass you by, for missed Timing can lead to missed results, happiness, and even true love.

Well, how does one know when the Timing is right?

By listening.

Listen to your intuition, your Higher Self during meditation, your Archangels and to God.

Pray or meditate daily and ask for guidance.

Listen for direction in life.

Be still and think.

These answers will come to you because we are all One. We all already know the best course of action. It is just a matter of tapping into it.

Learning God's Timing and trusting in his ability to bring the best to you all in his good Timing is a crucial part to mankind's Ascension and one of the many lessons we are here to learn.

You are quite capable of capturing the skills and abilities to do so.

Lesson 84 - Timing

Lesson 85 ᠂ Today

God intends for us to enjoy each and every day here on Earth.

Even when it's rainy and cold and we are burrowed snuggly into our homes, he intends for us to be grateful and love the day. For you have a warm and cozy abode to enjoy the clouds and raindrops. There will possibly be a rainbow.

The day as it unfolds is truly a miracle and we should embrace it. The rain brings precious water for our plants and trees and our food. Without the food, we would perish. Without the plants, the animals would go hungry. It's all interrelated. We need to look at the blessing of a rainy, cloudy, and cold day and be thankful.

Another reason to be thankful for such a gloomy day is so we can experience the dichotomy that occurs when we experience a sunny warm day.

We may think that is a "good" day, but all days do indeed have their benefits.

A cold or snowy day may result in time spent relaxing by a fire and reading a book to your youngsters or playing a game. Good family times could result. Whereas, if the weather were so called "nicer," all the children would be off attending to their own activities.

We must learn to cherish every day as special, for it truly is.

It is a day created for us by God: a wonderful gift.

Another day will never be the same.

Appreciate Today, the day God created just for you.

Appreciate the wonderful day he has blessed you with.

A key to Ascension is acknowledging and appreciating Today and every day.

Lesson 86 - Responsibility — The Layers

We all have layers of Responsibility that we carry with us on this journey.

We have Responsibility to ourselves to grow and learn and be the best we can be. The whole purpose for us being here is this reason.

Along the way, we are to learn other types of Responsibilities: how to care for our own families, our church or school or tribe, our community and eventually all of mankind.

Lastly, we are here to complete our Responsibilities to God by completing our mission or making progress on the steps towards it each lifetime.

Let us explain how: when you first arrive, you are a baby. You must learn how to thrive and survive. Hopefully, your parents take good care of you, but that's not always the case.

If you are not well-cared for, you need to survive. This might be *your* Responsibility, as overwhelming as it is for a baby or small child. You will likely cry to ask for food. Cry to ask for warmth and touch, and cry to have your diaper changed if you are uncomfortable. You will cry if your tummy hurts or you are cold or warm. This is how you notify the adults around you that you need care. This is *your* Responsibility, even as a baby.

As a small child and toddler, you also must rely on others for care and comfort. It's your Responsibility to let them know when things are not to your liking so they can correct it. Sometimes they will correct *you* instead. It is all part of the growing and learning process—both for you and for them.

As you grow, even as a child, you will learn Responsibility and teamwork, within your family unit. You will undoubtedly have some assignments required for the benefit of your family. This is how you learn Responsibility.

For example, in the preparation of meals, you may play a small part. As you grow into a teenager or young adult, you will eventually have Responsibility for preparing the entire meal. This is as God planned. It's your parent's Responsibility to teach you this. If they do not, then you should take it upon yourself, for the care of your body (through healthy meals) is and will be your Responsibility throughout the rest of your earthly life.

As you grow and go out on your own (and even before), you learn to be responsible to your team or your tribe. It could be a group activity, a sports team, or a religious group.

It doesn't matter what kind of group.

What matters is that you learn to accept Responsibility for your part and work together as one cohesive unit.

The process is then repeated with your spouse and later your children. It's incorporated into your expanding relationships with family—your own family, your parent's family, and your spouse's family.

You also tend to grow more responsible within your community and region. See how it expands?

As you learn and grow and accept more Responsibility, you take on more and more, and sense the Responsibility for all mankind.

In order to ascend, one must feel responsible for the wellness of all mankind.

"How can this be done?" you ask, "For it seems a monumental task."

Step by step is the way. Reason growth is so important.

If one only thinks about himself, he will not progress. If he is not responsible for his own life, his children, and his family, he will fail to be responsible for his tribe, community, or mankind.

Such an individual will make whatever feeble progress he can and will return to try again in another lifetime.

Some of us are rather slow learners. Much depends on our life circumstances—when and where we are born and who our first teachers (like our parents) were.

Some of us are stubborn and refuse to learn Responsibility in what others would deem an easier route—through loving parents setting an example.

Some learn best when they have a seemingly harder life, and others learn much on their own.

We each have our own ways of learning Responsibility, but eventually we all will become responsible for ourselves, our family, our community, and even mankind. It's part of the process and why we are all here.

Eventually, our learning and absorbing of Responsibility will set the stage for Ascension to the Heavens and our next stage of life.

Be well, be wise and try your best my children. I have the utmost of faith in you!

[Editor's Note: This seemed like a comment from God.]

Lesson 87 - **Confidence**

We must all learn to be confident if we are to be our best self, which is as God desires for us.

For only when we are our best self, can we do our best work—the work we are called to do. Once you know your life's work, your Confidence will help you soar to greatness in that pursuit.

How does one attain Confidence if you have none or an insufficient amount?

The answer is through lessons.

The answer is through stretching your comfortable boundaries.

The answer is through trials.

You see, after one has met great or difficult demands, one's Self-Confidence grows. Multiple trials, multiple demands—then even more Self-Confidence.

Coupled with positive self-talk, one can become unstoppable. One then addresses each situation with a strong sense of Confidence, of self-knowing as it were, that no obstacle is insurmountable.

Eventually any obstacle or hurdle will be viewed as such: an opportunity for growth or a chance to use one's skills to prove success.

Do not let obstacles and trials break you, for they are merely God's way of strengthening your inner core with lessons to overcome.

Even in times where it seems the "lesson" has gotten the better of us, remember we are still standing.

We are still breathing. So we have attained some measure of success, no matter how small. This tiny bit of success will lead to a tiny bit of Self-Confidence that will grow huge, beyond your imagination, with continued experiences.

Think of your Confidence as a small seed. Each new "lesson" is an opportunity for growth. Eventually your Confidence becomes a large, lush bush or tree ready to tackle any storm. Such as this your Confidence will be if you push yourself to continue learning lessons.

Your Confidence is an important attribute that you will need during your Ascension process, for the path to Higher Self is filled with challenges and opportunity for growth. One must develop high Self-Confidence in order to meet those challenges.

Lesson 88 - Wonderment

One must learn to look at life through the eyes of a child: in complete and utter Wonderment, for All That Is and all that can be.

This is definitely as God wishes. You see, he has created a most wonderful atmosphere, or setting, in which our lessons can take place. It is much like a classroom. A lovely classroom with millions of living and breathing beings (not just humans) for us to learn from and be exposed to.

Our Wonderment or curiosity will lead us to many lessons. We will be more open to learning if we first observe our environment and are thankful to God for creating such a place for us.

You see, when observing the Wonderment in nature, we can see how all things are interrelated. We can gain a sense of understanding about God.

Wonderment, in a sense, will lead us on the path of Ascension that God has planned for us.

Pay attention to the daily Wonder in your life and your journey will be swifter and more pleasant.

Not observing the Wonderment which surrounds us will lead to a bumpier journey and perhaps longer one.

It's up to each of us if we want to use the gifts God has placed before us to increase the enjoyment of our journey.

Lesson 88 - Wonderment

Lesson 89 - Adjectives

Adjectives are words used to describe someone or something: your selection of words in general is very important, but your selection of Adjectives is even more so.

You see, since whatever we believe will manifest itself in the physical world, so whatever descriptions we use tend to manifest themselves also.

Should we observe a cloudy day and say, "Oh it's a bad day, because it's cloudy," we will surely have a bad day.

But if on the other hand, we have the right mindset and say, "It is a beautiful cloudy day," and enjoy or realize the many benefits of such a day, our day will indeed be beautiful.

When we observe a child and say to him, "You are clumsy and stupid," it will undoubtedly become a self-fulfilling prophecy, for you will only see the clumsiness and stupidity in the child. But instead, if you say something encouraging and lift the child up, you will undoubtedly see quite a different outcome. Even using those descriptive Adjectives to define the child sends a message to his subconscious mind that "that" description IS him, so he acts accordingly.

Wouldn't it be so much better to use a positive and helpful Adjective? Wouldn't that lead to better growth and a more positive self-image of the child? Could it not change the trajectory of his life?

This is why words, especially Adjectives, are so very important.

One must learn to use words wisely in order to ascend, for ill thought-out words will lead on to hurt feelings, negative feelings, unwanted manifestations, and a much longer and tedious route to Enlightenment—a route that is unnecessary once we learn to choose our Adjectives more wisely.

Set a good example to others by your wise use of Adjectives. Your positivity will lift up others in ways you cannot even imagine. Your one kind remark with a special Adjective could be the one thing that propels another on their path to greatness, eventual Ascension. What a great gift to give another!

Lesson 90 - Persistence

Persistence in a time of sadness or grief is our topic today.

We will explain why one must go on even when one doesn't really want to.

We all have sad times and/or times of loss. They hit us hard. The pain is deep. We feel like no one else has ever endured such pain, yet we know that's not really true.

It just hurts so bad.

It seems unsurmountable. Yet it *is* surmountable with God, Jesus, the Divine, Source, Buddha, or whatever your chosen religious or spiritual leader is.

This is because we are all One. The other divine being(s) will carry you in your time of need. As you progress through this lifetime and others; you will/may eventually be in a place where you can lift up others too.

Think of this: you have a sad friend who experienced an event that made him cry, hurt his heart, and just left him feeling helpless. You observe him experience this pain. You go to him and offer comfort and friendship. You offer faith and goodwill. Eventually a smile cracks and he is on his way to a better day. One better day leads to other better days. See the difference you can make?

It's the same with those who turn to God to lift them up. God is One. We are all part of God. The same scenario occurs. God fills our heart with hope and love. Then we have the Persistence to carry on.

We must all lift each other up, even if it is just to remind each other we can be lifted to God for his healing and help.

Such actions will help us persevere through troubled times. For it is precisely those troubled times that will lead to our greatest growth. It is out of the darkness that we seek the light.

With the help of others, our spiritual basis, and our own free will, we can persist and make our way out of sadness and grief.

This is a lesson God plants in our paths so we can learn it. We need to be thankful for the lesson, for without darkness we aren't able to fully appreciate the light.

Think of these reasons. Think of these stories. For when you are experiencing the darkness, you will recall the reason why and the blessings to be derived.

Don't ever give up hope, for the answers are all within.

All we must do is seek the answers. Seek the truth and all will be known.

Important lessons to learn on our path to Ascension/Enlightenment.

Lesson 91 ⋅ Delaying Gratification

God wants us to have what we desire, but when we receive something we desire, it is all in God's timing. And His timing is perfect.

Some people think that if God can give us whatever we ask for, then we should receive it immediately. Yes, sometimes this does occur, but often it does not.

Take this example: a young woman wants a certain man, badly, and thinks he is her soulmate, her forever love. Yet, he does not appear to her quickly. She is unhappy and feels God has failed her.

Yet this is not the case. There could be a myriad of reasons.

We will explain two of them.

It's quite possible that her request is still in motion, for when she made her request, circumstances were not yet present for them to meet. Perhaps he has to travel a far distance for their paths to cross. Perhaps he is not yet the man of her dreams. Perhaps he or even she needs to grow more fully into spiritual beings before they meet.

Let's take another scenario. The woman is desiring a certain man she has identified as her soulmate, yet he doesn't come to her. Her advances are rebuffed, or he is with another. She is heartbroken, but indeed her soulmate *is* on his way to her. A more suitable gentleman is being formed—through his own growth process—that will someday come into her life.

You see, God, or the Universe, *does* hear our plans. He hears our requests, but *He* decides on the perfect timing as to when our wishes will be met.

By Delaying our Gratification, we learn many things.

First, we learn patience, which all humans need many trials to experience.

We learn faith. Faith in a higher being. Faith that what we wished (or something better) will come to us.

We learn to trust God or our higher power.

We exemplify these traits to others, and they learn from us. So we become teachers or followers that influence others.

Lastly, we grow and learn, which is the reason we are all here on Earth.

So you see, by Delaying Gratification, there are many rewards.

This is undoubtedly a lesson to be learned by all. A lesson quite necessary for Ascension.

Lesson 92 · Giving

Giving to others and Giving of oneself is an important lesson.

When we help others, we are Giving of our time, which we have a limited supply (seemingly). So we appear to be Giving away our time to help them. This is important, not only because we are all connected as One and should take care of our fellow man, but also important because of what Giving to others gives us in return.

We learn to be humble in the eyes of God.

We realize others are less fortunate than us.

We are grateful for our many blessings.

We are thankful for the opportunity to be of service to others.

It's the same when we give money, for we tend to think of money as a finite amount. We want to help, and this may be how we choose to do so. Hopefully, the funds will go to a worthy cause and help to lift up others in their plight.

No matter how we choose to do our Giving, it is important to note that while lives will be changed and enhanced by our Giving, the greatest benefit will be to *us*. For this is how we show our glory to God/Universe/Our Higher Spirit: that we are a learned being trying our best to move along the path to Ascension.

Those gifts will be returned to us tenfold.

You see, in the end, we are the recipients of all that we give, for we are truly Giving to our collective Oneness— One with All That Is.

A somewhat difficult concept to grasp, but we are sure with concentrated efforts one will be able to do so.

The important part to note is that your actions of Giving help all mankind, which in turn lifts you up, as you are part of mankind's collective consciousness.

Giving has an important role in lifting our consciousness. A necessary step in Ascension.

Lesson 93 ⋅ Hopelessness

We all have times when we feel Hopeless.

It may not be a pleasant feeling to experience, but we all do, nonetheless.

Why are we Hopeless? Why are we sad?

It's because we perceive we are without. Without love, without things we desire, without recognition, and without hope, basically. All the world seems against us, so it seems.

But this is just our *perception*, for all we need is already present. We just haven't accessed it, or the timing is not right. Or possibly there is an experience we must go through in order to grow and learn, and to advance to our next level.

"Do not give up hope my child," is what God admonishes us to do, for He will provide for our means.

When you are sad, think of it this way: as a passing phase that will eventually leave; a lesson can be learned during the time (however painful); our wishes or demands aren't always appropriate and God is saving us from additional, much worse pain, by not granting that wish at the time exactly as expected; and there is always more to the story or situation that we may not see or be aware of.

Think of Hopelessness as a phase that we grow through on our way to better, brighter days. It is just a little thorn in the rose to help us realize the real beauty of the journey.

There are ways to deal with one's Hopelessness.

You can seek answers within through prayer and meditation.

You can ask God to lift your worries, lift your spirit.

You can turn to friends and colleagues for encouragement and insight.

You can decide to wait till things change and they gradually will.

Do not despair. Do not fret. For this too will pass.

Someday you will look back at your life and realize your time of Hopelessness was merely a blimp on your timeline of life. A tiny blimp, which you indeed overcame.

Such is the lesson for Hopelessness. A lesson we must all learn on our path to Ascension.

Lesson 94 ⋅ Gems

A Gem in the weeds is our topic today.

"Whatever does this mean?" you might ask. It refers to finding the answer or the secret to the Universe. You see, the answer is right in front of us, hidden in the weeds. But we do not see the answer because we are too busy looking at the weeds!

Once we grow spiritually and start on our path of Enlightenment or Ascension, we learn to look beyond the weeds and seek the Gems hidden in the weeds. We learn to focus on the good, not the bad or messy or unpleasantness of life.

We learn to seek the Gems. In total, those very Gems hold the secrets to the Universe: why we are here, what we are here to learn, and what will become of us once we leave the Earth. All of God's (or Source's) plans will be revealed.

It takes effort.

It takes commitment.

It takes openness and free will.

One must be ready in mind, body, and spirit to hear and understand these lessons, for they are here (or hidden in the weeds) all along. Only when one is ready—which is defined as being on the correct vibrational frequency—is one able to access (or find) these Gems.

This is the reason we must remain open to learning and growing, for this is our mission here on Earth. As one advances, one learns and finds more Gems, so to speak. It is a journey we are all on, just at different crossroads on the path.

Some may not even be aware they are on the path, but merely incarnating here on Earth, puts one at the starting line of the path, as it were. When we are to hear the starting gun and let the race begin (again, so to speak) is totally up to our own awareness. Those not aware will stumble at the starting line or perhaps have a false start and not know where to go. Others will take off like a shot!

It matters not which methods one uses, for we will all go on the track eventually. The journey just takes longer for some than others.

Finding the Gems along the way, amidst the weeds, is part of the journey. How we respond to those Gems is what is significant and will lead us to greater understanding.

Do not be afraid to look for the Gems among the weeds, for they will assist in our very journey—the journey God/Universe has set in stone long before we set a humanly foot on this Earth.

Lesson 95 - Money

Money is a form of currency and nothing more. It helps with commerce—the buying and selling of goods, but it has no intrinsic value on its own. Piles and piles of it have no value except for gloating.

Why is that? Why is Money so valued in many cultures but the Money itself is worthless?

For it is only with what it can buy that we find its value. If a mother wants to feed her family, Money is most helpful. Money will help a cold, shivering child get a warm coat.

Yes, Money does have value—but in and of itself it holds none except what we as humans attach to it.

Can Money keep you warm at night?

Can Money comfort you when you are sad?

Can Money listen to your worries and lift them?

Can Money soothe your soul in times of loss or grief?

We think not. Money can, however, be of some use in aiding those symptoms. It can buy a method of heat with a house and that will keep you physically warm, but your heart may remain untouched.

Money can buy "things" that may momentarily lift your sadness.

Money can buy time with a therapist you can tell your worries to, but they will only help you see solutions within. They will not take your troubles away.

Money cannot cure soul issues, for those are also found within.

You see how Money is only useful as a tool to help attain what we need or desire. And, notably, we cannot buy everything we do so desire.

Can you buy love? Well, it might seem so to the man whose woman swoons when he buys her a big diamond ring, a fancy house, and a luxury car. She will hang on his every word. Yet if he loses everything, will she stay by his side? If it was the Money, or the items purchased with Money, that attracted her to him, she will likely find a better suitor.

So you see, Money—although seemingly—can buy love, it is only an illusion, for true and lasting love is derived from the soul, not through things purchased with Money.

As you grow and learn on your journey, we hope at some time this lesson, this very important lesson, will sink in and be absorbed. For God wants all beings to learn about the value of Money—what it is and what it is not.

This important step in our development will lead to our mutual growth and Ascension.

One day there will be no need for Money, for man will learn how to obtain all that he and she desire without Money.

Some people are using this method already.

Some people are starting to open up to the possibility.

Others remain close-minded to the possibility.

We will discuss this method—called manifesting—in more detail another day.

Suffice it to say, the lesson we are to learn about Money is that it alone does not buy happiness. Helping others to realize this once *we* have learned this lesson is part of our own growth process too, for others learn by example.

As you learn, remember to serve as that shining example, in this lesson as well as others.

Lesson 95 - Money

Lesson 96 - Loneliness

Today we will discuss Loneliness and how to cope in times of isolation or feeling isolated.

First of all, we all feel lonely at some time or another, whether we think so or not. Some people are more sensitive to being alone because they haven't built up defense mechanisms or ways to cope with it.

Let us explain: take a child who grows up as an only child versus one who grows up with many siblings. The only child will learn how to occupy himself from an early age because he has to. The child from a big family never has a moment's peace and may not even know what it feels like to be alone, even for a moment, for he never has the opportunity to experience such a thing.

Both experiences are a gift.

Both experiences require growth into understanding the opposing viewpoint.

Then there are all the many situations of upbringing in between...half siblings, combined families, smaller families, broken families and so forth. Each situation brings its own lessons and trials. Each situation allows for our growth and may leave plenty of room for additional growth on the other spectrum.

We must use these experiences to learn to grow in many ways, including how to grow in Loneliness.

We should never be afraid to be alone, for we are never truly alone. It is our *perception* of being alone and *feeling* alone that can be upsetting.

You see, we are never truly alone, for God or our Holy Spiritual Leader is always with us. We must learn to lean on Him in troubled times when Loneliness takes over.

We need to redirect our thoughts and feelings to being One with our creator and all the other beings (living and deceased). Once we can master such an outlook, our feelings will coincide, and we will never be lonely again.

Another way to look at being alone—at least in the physical nearby sense—is that such "quiet" time is truly a gift.

It's a gift to be enveloped in quiet time for self-reflection and self-growth. You can learn a lot if you just sit quietly and talk to yourself! You will astound yourself with the headway you can make on problems or issues if you just take your own advice much like you would from an old friend.

Being alone, especially in nature, is a great way to become aware of the beauty of our planet and All That Is. Sometimes when too many people are around us, we are distracted and do not enjoy or absorb all the beauty that surrounds us.

Many lessons are to be learned from Loneliness, so do not despair and fall victim to only the unpleasant side of it, for being Lonely can truly be a blessing!

Nonetheless, it is one of the feelings we must master and learn from in order to ascend or become enlightened.

One last comment: when you observe others being lonely, it is your responsibility to try to comfort them and help them see the joys of being lonely as we just mentioned, for we are all here to learn and grow *and* help each other do so when called to assist them.

Lesson 97 ‒ Children

Children are truly a gift from God.

This is something we all must learn to know and appreciate, for it is a great gift indeed.

The purpose of Children is not only a means of our spiritual beings' arrival on Earth, but it is a way to teach others many, many of life's lessons.

Take for instance the parents of this dear Child. They will learn about miracles when they create a new life. Many will be in awe of the magnificent accomplishment, as they should be. They will learn responsibility (whether or not they accept their responsibility is another thing) but they will be presented with the *opportunity* to do so.

The parents will learn to be teachers, either on purpose or by default. For if they fail to teach their Children or teach them well, the Children will observe their actions/inactions and it shapes their perception of parenting.

Parents learn to be strong and love hard when they have Children.

They learn to try harder than they would otherwise in life.

For some, having Children is the catalyst for transformation of themselves to a much better life, a better person, and one with high consciousness.

So you see, Children have a great impact on their parents and their parent's development.

Let's take the other family relationships. If there are other Children in the family, they will learn to share. They'll have to share food, toys, and parent's attention. They may be too young to understand the concept of sharing money, but that is precisely what they will share as parents (most of them, anyway) do have a limited amount of funds to spend on their family. When Johnny needs a new pair of shoes, Susie might not be able to get a new dress and so forth.

Most certainly Children will learn to share their parent's time, for it is limited. If father is only available three hours in the evening before bedtime, the Children may clamor to his knees and he will attempt to console or visit with them. Yet if one Child has special needs or the mother has needs, the Children may be put on the back burner.

Such is the balance of life. Children will learn to value time with their parents as they grow, for that special time together is limited. It's only a fleeting glimpse on the timeline of our lives.

Children bring joy to the extended family as well. Just by being born, they create grandparents who then must step into this new role, whether they are ready or not. So in this way, Children do indeed spur the growth of elders. Quite amazing if you think about it.

Grandchildren have been known to mend families to at least a place of cordiality because of divorce or division in the past. Nothing will keep a grandparent from their grandchild, even old wounds from previous spouses.

It can truly be a miracle—or a gift, you see—how Children can bring a family together.

The same scenario goes for extended family members. Once Children come into the picture, siblings rethink the importance of family and tend to want the cousins to meet and know each other.

Children are the very ties of a family. They are what binds it together. Seeing generation after generation grow and know each other is a true blessing, especially to the patriarch and matriarch of the families.

So now we hope you see and understand the many blessings of Children and how and why they are considered gifts from God.

Lesson 98 - Simplicity

The role of Simplicity in our lives is paramount.

You see, as we learn and grow, we start to realize that Simplicity is the key to making great strides and moving ahead quickly.

You see, if we have too many "things" occupying our time, we cannot maintain direction or focus on the things that are really important.

Simplicity in our lives helps us maintain focus.

When we are distracted by a myriad of little things, we are unable to concentrate on the bigger things, those things paramount to the big picture and further development of our souls. We get lost in the weeds, so to speak.

So when one is designing their life, it is best to keep this in mind. Simplicity breeds focus, which then—if it becomes a habit—will lead to greatness. This is a very important trait or ideal to master.

You see, when our lives are a mess, scattered all around us, without focus, we can barely get by.

Our aim cannot be directed to the things or actions that mean the most and will help us advance the most quickly.

If one wants to grow and truly advance at the quickest pace, one must learn how to separate the wheat from the chaff, so to speak, and pare down one's responsibilities and commitments to the simplest form possible in order to concentrate or put forth effort on the important tasks at hand—the ones that will indeed move yourself and mankind forward.

This is as God or our Great Creator intends. The process takes eons as it is: without Simplicity it will take even longer.

Think about these suggestions and try your best to meld them into your daily structure and you will see great results, because remember:

$$FOCUS + HABIT \rightarrow RESULTS$$

Simplicity is simply a way to accomplish the *focus* portion of this equation.

Great leaders master this habit; that is why they have the time and focus to become great. We all can be great in our way and this is a method to obtain greatness.

Lesson 99 - Organization

The skill of Organization is something we all must bring into our lives also.

For how are we to get our lives on track and concentrate on the most important of tasks if we are amidst a pile of disorganization?

Sometimes disorganization is in the physical sense, which we can all relate to: messes around our home, office, or yard; things not put away or not put away in an organized fashion. (See how simplicity would help here?)

Nonetheless, we can all easily see how lack of Organization and the ensuing mess can keep us from concentrating or focusing on what is important.

There is the mental or psychological disorganization too, where thoughts are jumbled and not cohesive. We have to work within ourselves to have a more consolidated and organized brain, if you will.

First, we'll explain what we mean by this and then give examples to help deal with it. A disorganized mental state is when your thoughts are all over the place. "I should do this; no, I shouldn't do this. I want this; no, I don't want this. I'm pretty; no, I'm not pretty." In other words, conflicting thoughts that are opposing to each other.

Then there is the situation where you have way, way too many thoughts. We all have many thoughts, even at the same time, and they are too numerous to even count. But this is an even higher number of thoughts that is so all-consuming that our brain literally stalls like a vehicle when it is flooded with gas. You or your brain is unable to cope. This is too many thoughts at once.

This too can be an overwhelming problem. The way to deal with this issue is to practice calming the mind, so fewer thoughts come and go at once, so it is at least at a manageable level.

Some call this meditation or concentrated breathing. Others practice yoga and receive the same results. If you are afflicted with a racing and congested mind, by all means seek solutions and work towards resolving this resistance type of behavior if you want to move ahead in life, for it is quite necessary.

If your mind has the conflicting thoughts, then you too will need to work towards calming your mind. The difference is that during your "calming session," you must ask your Higher Self what you really want.

Do you want to be pretty or not pretty? Do you want to be happy or not happy? Choose your path and keep that thought alone, so as to draw that action to you. Concentrate on what you want and reiterate it in your mind over and over until it is one cohesive thought on that topic, not opposing views or choices.

In essence, train your mind for what you *want*. In essence, organize your mind the way you want it.

Once your mental thoughts and physical surroundings are properly organized, you will be better equipped to make great strides in your journey and therefore learn and grow as God/Our Creator intended. But it starts within us and with the desire to do the work necessary to accomplish what we desire. If we aren't willing to look within and figure out how to set the stage for our growth, then we will remain stagnant.

Organizing our life and our minds are important steps not only for enhancing our journey and getting us on the path, but it also helps others. You see, they are always observing us and learning through us and deciding what actions to take themselves.

In a sense we are all leading others. Another reason to be organized…to set us on the path and to set a good and worthy example for others to follow.

Lesson 100 - The Miracle

It is truly a Miracle, one for all mankind to behold: that which we are here to learn and grow, and that our great Creator has envisioned and created this wonderful playground, known as Earth, for us to carry out our activities.

When you think about the grand picture of life itself and all that goes into a carefully synchronized set of activities, all intertwined with exact precision, to accomplish the mere feat of creating our lovely oasis, it can only be described as nothing short of a Miracle!

That God so loved us—eternal spiritual beings—that he created an atmosphere so conducive to our growth, is really beyond our wildest imaginations.

But it is true, and we must embrace this Miracle—the Miracle of our own creation and the creation of our Earth and our Universe as part of a divine plan, where we are merely cogs in the wheels of time, moving things forward for all mankind.

Someday, and someday soon (however, not in human terms) the lessons will be learned, the challenges met, and we will all unite as one cohesive unit and ascend to the Heavens above to be reunited with our Creator, only to repeat the exercise in a newly-created location, just as lovely as this one.

This will be a repeating pattern through eternity where we learn and grow infinitely in time, for there is always more to learn.

There is always more to know.

With the help of God and other Ascended Masters, we can all make this journey through time and dimensions, reaching higher levels of consciousness along the way.

For ours is a great gift bestowed on us: that of living and learning through eternity.

This is the Miracle that our Great Creator has bestowed on us.

Let us not waste this great Miracle.

Let us put our best efforts into this endeavor.

Let us learn the lessons.

Let us grow to be all we can be.

Then let us learn and grow again so the cycle is repeated, and we become all that we can be.

This is as God planned. So it shall be.

What is "The New I AM Document?"

These are a group or set of discourses designed to help mankind and lift them up to a new way of thinking so as to aid in their enlightenment and growth.

You see, "I AM" means we are One.

You are One with me and I am One with you.

Individually and together, we are One with God.

We are all already connected, but it appears we are separate.

By learning and understanding the lessons in these discourses—this one, Volume I, and the other two to follow—mankind will be led to another level of understanding.

For this reason, "The New I AM Document" and following discourses are most important for the development and eventual Ascension and Enlightenment of mankind.

Your dear comrade [Editor's Note: The speakers are referring to Janie J] has diligently transcribed these words for your benefit.

Although some may doubt her abilities, we assure you she has been most diligent and faithful in carrying out her responsibilities for this task.

Keep this in mind when you want to reach out in ridicule.

Think about why would she do such a thing for your benefit unless she was compelled to do so? Keep your doubts to yourself and do not infect others with your naysaying. Someday you will come around and realize it *is* all true.

For those hearty learners, eager to delve into the mysteries of mankind, here is your opportunity. Listen and learn my friends. Adopt these lessons to your lives. Absorb the meanings into your soul and live the life God has imagined for us all.

It is a freeing life.

It is a beautiful life.

It is a never-ending life, one we will all accomplish together one day.

Let's start on the path now.

Be peace. Be love. Be the light.

Namaste.

Your Eternal Spirit Guides and Ascended Masters.

Afterword

This book may seem simple to some and too outrageous for others, however its meaning can be absorbed by all. By reading and reflecting on these lessons, one can put them into practice. If one lives by these lessons, one will serve as a great example to others.

One can teach their children or others these timeless lessons by reading as a group, reflecting, and leading a discussion. We all need encouragement, and this book contains many lessons for our lifetime that we can use to encourage ourselves and others.

There are to be two additional discourses—Volume II and Volume III—although the timing is not yet known. Rest assured though; it will be in God's perfect timing.

Afterword

About the Author

Janie Jurkovich (known as Janie J) is an author, nationally ranked athlete, world traveler, and a spirit medium.

After experiencing a divorce in her sixties, Janie J set about reinventing her life to achieve some semblance of harmony and happiness. The result? She wrote her first books to encourage and remind women that it is never too late to live their best lives.

She honed her ability to tap into her intuition and the spirit world along the way. She soon realized that spirituality was indeed part of living one's best life.

After embracing her "gift" of connecting to souls in other realms, she committed her life to helping others by sharing what she has learned. Her life goal is to help lift the consciousness of all mankind.

Janie J lives in the country near Clovis California with her dog Pepper, a brood of hens and a flock of sheep. It's a tranquil setting which allows her to connect to the spirit world so she can live her life's purpose.

The New I AM Document, Volume I, is Janie J's sixth book.

For more information visit:
www.TheNewIAmMovement.com

About the Author

Join The New I AM Movement

Are you ready to change your life for the better?

Are you ready to upgrade your existence?

Are you ready to help move mankind to a higher level of consciousness that is in line with what our Creator envisioned?

It all starts with YOU!

If you are ready to take the next step on this spiritual journey, find out how to get these lessons so you can grow into a *better person* and become a *more evolved spiritual being*.

Go to www.TheNewIAmMovement.com

Just imagine being a part of this extraordinary movement—a movement to move mankind ahead to new, higher levels of understanding and consciousness. Such a noble feat is quite possible if we work *together* to make this happen!

Join The New I Am Movement as you work on your own spiritual development. Connect to me, to others, your higher self and with your Spirit Guides, Ascended Masters, and Universal Intelligence. We are all available to help you on your spiritual journey.

CPSIA information can be obtained
at www.ICGtesting.com
Printed in the USA
LVHW052302080122
708077LV00007B/173

9 781736 947630